Susan Dunker Public Library
and the Dover Public Library

Bonne chance!

Simone Dutil Massie

12-17

Growing Up
Franco-American

(with no black patent-leather shoes)

LORRAINE DUTILE MASURE

~ Dedication ~

To my grandparents,
Elmire Beauchesne Côté and Joseph Côté,
the original dreamers,
whose courageous odyssey to this wonderful country
flourished into cherished reveries of the good life

To my parents,
Lauretta Côté Dutile and Wilfred Joseph Dutile, Sr.,
fiddlers on the roof,
whose Old World traditions imbued our lives
with the rich texture of mission and harmony

To Jackie
who lovingly listened to parts of this
humble *oeuvre* over and over again...

To Chris:
Had he traveled my journey, because of his literary talent,
this *memoir* would read more like a classic

To Carl and Janice Longfellow:
While he prodigally dispensed his sunny inspiration,
it was she who planted the seed, the idea, of this humble
endeavor...

Growing Up Franco-American
(with no patent-leather shoes)
was paraphrased countless times by the author
at guest-speaking presentations,
across Southern Maine and New Hampshire.

Herewith some of the reviews:
"Growing up Franco..." is a poignant, eloquent, touching
and hilariously funny presentation. Content could be
applied to any ethnicity. Just change the menus and
location. Not just for Francos but fun for all.
I encourage you to see this show."
- Anna Ashley, Producer
Nasson College Alumni
Association
Cultural and Educational Programs

"Masure's lecture brimmed with memories."
- Tammy Wells, Journalist
[York County, Maine*] Journal-Tribune*

"A fantastic evening enjoyed by all."
- Patrons Barbara and Fred Boyle

"At the conclusion of her presentation, she received
a standing ovation from the capacity crowd."
- Dr. Morton Gold, Reviewer
[York County, Maine] *Journal-Tribune*

"A lovely souvenir of the past."
- Patron Irene Roberge

~ Contents ~

~Introduction~

~ Introduction ~

A Celebration of Culture!

BECAUSE OF BOTH "inspiration and perspiration" the essence of this book was already composed, lying there on discrete Power Point pages that continue to be prompting points for various oral presentations given by the author. Further, many who had come to listen might have finished some of my sentences due to their own colorful and exotic Franco connections given the proximity of their homes in either New Hampshire or Maine to the Province of Quebec. My own supplemental oral interjections about Franco *gestalt* have connected these slides and served me and audiences well.

If I were to convey to readers now the honest portrait of what was essentially an Old World upbringing, it was necessary to transfer those Power Point pictures to the blank canvas of this book's pages, not painting by numbers, but instead liberally splashing color linkages to incubate the journey. (We're French for crying out loud!) My mission, as I saw/see it, is to become a cultural tour guide who escorts the reader along my cherished (and not so cherished) memories.

This story is about what it was really like growing up as a first-generation American with a rich Franco heritage — across the multiple venues of home, family, church, school, and other settings as seen through the admittedly slanted paradigms of yesterday's youth and of today's octogenarian lens. A clear advantage is that my immigrant mother who prodigally furnished me with folklore lived 94 years, and that I am currently 83 years of age. That's a lot of history!

Given the current topical and frequent media allusions to the subject of immigration, it was tempting to imbue the book's title with a fetching immigration-related hook. But that would feel fraudulent. Although it *was* the immigration of my grandparents that spawned most of this story, it is more essentially about our culture: the behaviors and beliefs characteristic of our particular social, ethnic, or age group. Moreover, its furthest objective is to seem a manual for aspiring happily-ever-after migrants. I confess that this book's actual title has been plagiarized, in part, from the John R. Powers novel, "Do Black Patent Leather Shoes Really Reflect Up?" My Franco tribe has never subscribed to the theology that hell is paved with good patent leather shoes, but I did conclude with the ulterior motive that the title might attract readers from all walks of life. (No pun intended.)

I am aware that some readers may resent the adjectival term "Franco" or "African" American, preferring rather that all this country's citizens refer to themselves as simply "Americans." Understood. If you are offended by such a term,

I ask you to continue reading while suspending judgment until I have painted the last dab on this portrait.

At some of my Power Point presentations about growing up Franco-American, both grandmothers or mémères have kindly escorted youngsters to the event in order for them to gain a sense of history about living relics like me! The reactions have been diverse, but one conclusion remains clear: some of the experiences described here are generational as well as cultural. To be sure, seniors of all heritages may well see themselves in my stories. And young people are usually amazed at how quaint (that's code for "wicked") life was then for many of us old-timers. To these I say, I have been your age; remember that you have never been 83!

---

* Title cobbled from John R. Powers' novel, *Do Black Patent Leather Shoes Really Reflect Up?* (Regnery 1975)

I

Historical Background (Stuffy Stuff)

O canada terre de nos aieux...[*]

— Adolphe-Basile Routhier
et Calixa Lavallée

---

[*] *(Oh, Canada, land of our forefathers...)*

~ Historical Background ~

ISTORY INFORMS THAT two reasons loom large as to why the Great Migration of the French from Canada to the United States primarily in the 19th and 20th Centuries occurred.

The first, you might have guessed, involved war which usually includes territory. In 1759 the British finally prevailed over the French, winning The Battle of Quebec. Commonly known is that the conflict between the British and the French in Europe long predated the actual Canadian setting of that Quebec battle on The Plains of Abraham. And to this day, the insistence of the French language over the English in that Province is without doubt the corroborating conviction of a people who believe they were then treated by the British as second-class citizens. I note the assertion on Quebec's automobile registration plates: *Je me souviens* (I remember) although historians ascribe it to a wider sentiment of grievances.

Second, it was nothing less than the epic and distant event called the Industrial Revolution in England one-half Century earlier that made possible and probable my own grandparents' emigration from the Province of Quebec in Canada to Lewiston, Maine in the United States.

The word "revolution" (and all of its permutations) is well-cast here. I speak of that very dynamic, powerful, and comprehensive period mid-19th Century that brought about a climactic transformation at once world-wide and in most arenas of individual life: *when manual labor evolved into the Mechanical Age.*

Scottish philosopher Thomas Carlyle (1795 – 1891) strongly believed it to foreshadow marginalized individual aspiration:

> Were we required to characterize [*sic*] this age of ours by any single epithet, we should be tempted to call it, not an Heroical, Devotional, Philosophical, or Moral Age, but, above all others, the Mechanical Age…The shuttle drops from the fingers of the weaver, and falls into iron fingers that ply it faster…There is no end to machinery. For all earthly, and for some unearthly purposes, we have machines and mechanic further-ances; for mincing our cabbages; for casting us into magnetic sleep. We war with rude Nature; and, by our resistless engines, come off always victorious, and loaded with spoils.

Why did the Mechanical Age originate in England? Because she had everything going to complement its growth — natural and financial resources from her slave colonies, especially benefiting from slave trade between Africa and the Caribbean; she was considered "Queen of the Seas" with a commanding Navy and ships to transport goods; favored with a dense population for its small size, she enjoyed a stable political situation — a monarchy and rule of law; most of all, England had the willingness to change and a dynamic Protestant work ethic to implement it all.

The Norton Anthology of English Literature reports that England experienced an enormous increase in wealth, but rapid and unregulated industrialization brought a host of social and economic problems. In Canada, due to a sudden growth in population of British loyalists, families could not support themselves due to law and systems, but also because the new British leaders of Canada reserved land for the English and English systems of colonization. Additionally there was also the "Château Clique" which ruled the Province of Quebec, blocking expansion of housing and land development with the result that French Canadians were not allowed enough land for shelter. Meanwhile, New England was industrializing, and its promise was tantalizingly close, just south of the border.

To peasants such as my grandparents, Elmire Beauchesne Côté and Joseph Côté, the Mechanical Age held a life-changing, transformative opportunity! The creation of machine tools and the factory, mostly in nearby New England because of fast-running rivers for water power, provided a vision of the good life in America. (With steam power invented after the Civil War, the Industrial Revolution did spread across all of the United States. Cities were formed, people migrated to factories.)

One such factory was The Bates Mill, a textile factory company founded in 1850 and located at 35 Canal Street in Lewiston, Maine. Mill #1 was completed in 1852. Benjamin Bates built the mill in Lewiston close to its location at Lewiston Falls, which initially provided power to the mill. The Mill was operated by water power from the Androscoggin River and combined power spinning and weaving on looms. The Mill produced textiles until the 21st century. Thousands of immigrants from Canada and Europe immigrated to Lewiston to gain employment at the mills. My grandmother was among them.

The magnitude of the huge migration (*la grande hemorragie*) shook Quebec society since most of the immigrants came from rural areas of Quebec. They were seeking financial and job security, especially in textile and shoe factories. And why not? They could do so by traveling a relatively short distance for a brand-new life!

According to one estimate, a million Quebecois emigrated to the Northeast between 1820 and 1920, most to work in textile and paper mills, shoe factories, and the like. Many more were woodcutters such as my grandfather. Although such moves generally led to better lives, they were not made without pain. In his short story *Germaine,* Denis Ledoux captures the distress of the main character as she and her husband and children leave their hardscrabble farm in Quebec for factory jobs in Maine where:

They would have more money in the States because they would work in a mill. Every week they would receive a paycheck — whether there was a cold snap or not, whether there was rainfall or not. Nonetheless, Germaine wonders, how were they going to survive in a place where what they knew wasn't what you had to know, and, as their farmhouse disappeared from view, she burst into tears.

Conflicted in their quest, they were well aware that they had little formal education, they did not even know how to speak the English language, had little understanding of industrialization, and had never lived under a democracy. Their birth certificates attested to this since they were both classified as "British."

Later, they would come to know insidious prejudice. As example, upset with mostly Catholic immigrants, the Klu Klux Klan surfaced some dozen years after they arrived in 1912. Laurie Meunier in her book, *On Being Franco-American* writes:

At work a co-worker told my father that he would rather have his daughter marry an African-American than a Catholic. Except he didn't say it that politely. Later still, I learned about the Klu Klux Klan's history in Maine, and how their targets were primarily Catholic Franco-Americans. In 1920 Maine's population was 768,000. Only four short years later, membership in the Maine Klu Klux Klan was 50,000 and growing.

Paul Doiron (editor *emeritus* of *Down East Magazine*) in an article entitled "Lingua Franca" (Assimilation shouldn't mean leaving your language behind) writes of his dad:

> There were other reasons to leave his heritage behind. Kids with names like Pelletier and Michaud might find it hard to believe that Franco- Americans were, until very recently, forbidden to eat at certain Maine restaurants and stay at certain Maine inns. That particular discriminatory era predates ours (although discrimination is still a sad fact of life for many in this country). But I am old enough to remember being the subject of mean-spirited "frog" jokes.

It could be said that even to this day biased commentators (Alan Haley: "Demographics, xenophobia aren't working in our state's favor," April 11, 2016, *Portland Press Herald*) describe immigration differently according to who was immigrating:

> In 1820, Maine became the first state to constitutionally guarantee citizenship to the thousands of forced immigrants from Africa living in America. We were so proud of that one act that we chose "I lead" as our state motto.

However, Mr. Haley has a different take that is only inferentially positive about Franco-Americans seeking citizenship, at best as economic assets:

> Starting in the 1900s, Maine was overrun by immigrants who spoke a foreign language, practiced a strange religion and who were believed at the time to be dirty, of low moral character and intelligence and owing allegiance to a foreign power. They were, of course, the French Canadians. Owen Brewster, our 54th governor, was elected in 1925 with the help of Maine's Klu Klux Klan, on the very specific promise to keep this "popish" element in its place and send them back to Canada at the first opportunity. There was nothing special or cultural about the economic surge French Canadians provided — it was just the natural result of thousands of people purchasing thousands of products and services, providing thousands more products and services in return and paying taxes on it all.

These original dreamers *were* generally noted for their neatness (see 3. A La Maison), and sought passionately to improve their life, yes, paying taxes, learning the language, and adhering to all of the laws that applied to them. They too held a strong work ethic, and they were blessed with Emerson's uncommon sense and good will.

But the positive aspects of relocating clearly eclipsed the prejudice: The factory had such an impact on the world itself that President Calvin

Coolidge once wrote, "Everyone who builds a factory builds a temple."

Whether to work or to worship, my grandparents were ready for the Adventure!

2

Personally Speaking

Father, Mother, and Me,
Sister and Auntie say
All the people like us are We,
And everyone else is They.

— RUDYARD KIPLING

~ Personally Speaking ~

"**L**'état, c'est moi," ("The State is Me") asserted Louis IV in 1661. Not exactly what my maternal grandparents could — or would have wanted to — boast although "L'état du Maine est à moi" ("The State of Maine is mine") would have aptly described their situation in 1912. Even though they had infrequently visited the States, they permanently emigrated from Saint Fabian, Rimouski, Province de Quebec that year with nine children and one on the way when my mom was 16 months old.

It is that very paragraph that endorses me as a first-generation American!

(My paternal grandparents were born in Cranbourne – pépère - and Sacré Coeur de Marie - mémère -, Quebec.)

Our large, emigrating Côté ancestors entered the country through Island Pond, Vermont, finally arriving at the Grand Trunk Railway Station in Lewiston, Maine. Island Pond had become an important railroad center in 1853 when the Grand Trunk Railway established international connections between Montreal, Canada, and several Maine cities including

Lewiston. The station, located at the corner of Lincoln and Beech Streets, was built in 1874 by the Lewiston and Auburn Railroad Company and leased to the Grand Trunk Railway. Many French-Canadian immigrants arrived in the Lewiston-Auburn area via the station, causing the building to be known as the "Ellis Island" of Lewiston.

They left an agrarian way of life that included farming and woodcutting to put down roots (or perhaps the literal opposite) in this country at a time when The Mechanical Age excitedly beckoned. And although their remote vision of the good life was likely, romantically glossed over in technicolor hues, their reasoning of a guaranteed paycheck from the mills and textile places that glowingly tantalized them — as opposed to the fickle outcomes of farming dependent on weather and crops — was soundly steeped in reality.

Like most of her siblings, my mom left school in the fifth grade because she had no shoes. This physical lack of shoes also tied in "nicely" with the gender-tilted philosophy of the-then Franco-American culture that "you don't need to go to school to learn to change diapers." Further, by being at home she would be free to help with babysitting and discharging chores while her mother toiled in the Bates Mills.

All of my mother's siblings were known by a second name, and this, due to human habit, to their dying day. The reason? Once they had some height, their parents would send away for a Canadian cousin's birth certificate allowing them to fib they were of legal age (16) to work in the Lewiston textile mills or bleacheries.

My dad from Laconia, New Hampshire and my mom met at her sister's home in Lewiston where my father boarded. They fell in love, married in 1933, but had very little in common except for the most important endowment in any relationship: the shared values of hearth, family, and faith.

Dad's approach to life was somewhat scientific or you might say methodical: he knew exactly how many seconds it should take to button a shirt or how many steps there were from the kitchen where he sliced the meat micrometrically to, say, his bedroom where he did not so much arrange as align his bedclothes. Seldom one for change, there was no soap like Camay, no toothpaste like Colgate, and no deodorant like Mum. It is difficult to paint him on this piece of paper. For, if he could be scientist, so could he be poet. Lover of surprises, birthdays and Christmases were first-class feasts, high holidays prefaced by much anticipation and whispering, culminating into a swirling, rushing and ha! ha! of the colors of his life. I recall as well sparkling, brilliant Necco circles of Sunday afternoon car rides through country woods he regarded as majestic! White and even whiter birches were his favorite, and he would point them out as we rode, with exclamation and childlike simplicity. Three of us, then, in the backseat would always begin these Sunday afternoon rides fighting "for a side." Usually, we would sing on the way home: English, French, Latin songs. "Home" meant Krispy Crackers smothered in hot, delicious home-made soup for supper (*souper*): pasta, tomatoes, onions, leftover roast beef (now cubed) from lunch.

Mom, on the other hand, was an incurable romantic who also loved music, but as well theatre and the movies. How idyllic a world this centerpiece of our Shaker-clean home composed for us: delectable patés and soufflés with no recipe to speak of ("you just take a little pinch of xxx and throw it in"), player-piano dusks, Strauss, Picasso, Emily Post *de rigeur*, starched or pressed home-made clothing, Rodgers & Hammerstein wake-up calls to the smell of warm cinnamoned coffee cake. With a little paint, a few yards of cloth, and her keen sense of comeliness, she could transform a gingham tenement into a taffeta manor. All the many years we were growing up, I never saw my mother lie down during the day. And I never saw my dad lie down at the end of day without physically kneeling in prayer, leaning against an upholstered chair in our parlor.

Of course they sometimes had their differences of opinion and arguments, but never the loss of respect. She could be incredibly comical without realizing it. Or did she? It was she who counseled my teenage son, "Mémère don't care for that pre-mental sex stuff." And once, after my dad had made quite a complimentary comment about some well-shaped woman, she (who too read her English newspaper faithfully every day, but didn't always transcribe the text to the proper phonetics) turned to me with all seriousness in her cryptic French brogue and said, "Your father thinks he's a Don Jo Anne."

I was born at home since we couldn't afford a hospital or a doctor. My mémère was the mid-wife, and at 1:55 pm, Thursday, September 27, 1934 in Lewiston during a thunderstorm so violent it knocked out the electricity, I appeared. My mother had been anesthetized with chloroform and awoke to lighted candles that provoked her to think she had been given the last rites of the Church. (Yikes…)

It was critical in those days, according to that same Church, that a baby be baptized as soon after birth as possible lest s/he be banished to limbo, the supposed abode of the souls of unbaptized infants. And so I was carried to Holy Cross Church on Lisbon Street in Lewiston at the tender age of 2.5 days. Mothers seldom attended the brief ceremony since, it was understood, they were usually recuperating from the blessed event. (Oxymoron there?) Present were the father and, of course, grandparents who promised to rear the child in the faith should parents be unable to.

Yes, it was an idyllic childhood. With four brothers as my siblings, there was ample opportunity for tricks that went both ways. My favorite was, say, approaching my brother, Richard, outdoors one day and challenging his prowess: "Bet you can't pee outside." His male pride caused an automatic response of his male equipment, resulting in a glorious arc of liquid. His thoughts of victory were soon vanquished though when I immediately bolted in the house and hollered, "Hey, mom; Richard peed outside."

All of us knew our lane. Each of us had their role. Indeed, happy days!

Given the chosen organization/sequencing of this *ethnic memoir* (*venues* emphasizing culture rather than chronology stressing narrative), I now take license to fast-forward seven years all the way to 1941.

Like many Americans my age, I remember as though it was yesterday the day the Japanese bombed Pearl Harbor. I was seven years old, and my parents tuned the large Philco console radio to President Roosevelt's address, lamenting the international announcement. Was there ever more American resolve and patriotism before or since? There seemed to be sacrifice woven in most aspect of our lives: rationing of many goods; saved tinfoil and scrapmetal; tissue paper mail from our armed forces; victory gardens; saved fat for glycerin to make bullet powder; redesigned men's woolen suits with narrower lapels and no pants cuffs to conserve wool for military uniforms; at home, air raid drills and wailing sirens behind drawn shades. Everything possible to feed and arm our troops. Given my youth, I cannot be certain there was no dissent about the big WWII (as Archie Bunker used to call it), but in retrospect it sure feels as though there was little.

Eleanor Roosevelt challenged Hollywood producers to "keep 'em laughing." Not surprisingly, movies drew 90 million viewers a week in 1944 out of a total population of 132 million people. It seemed as though everyone went to the movies. As well as to church.

The end of the war in 1945 saw the American people's continued solidarity exploding in an unbelievable national celebration! Sad that President Roosevelt's death a few months earlier prevented his witnessing such a global victory for the country he and we so loved…

3

À La Maison*

*Mid pleasures and palaces though we may roam,
Be it ever so humble there's no place like home!*

— JOHN HOWARD PAYNE

---

* AT HOME

~ À La Maison ~

Until WWII and within the fierce pride of their Americanization, the descendants of the Quebecois emigrants are reputed to have preserved their identity better than did most other ethnic groups. "Little Canada's" were established in some districts of towns and cities as they attempted to maintain and reproduce the native culture of their families and organizations. Parts of these enclaves survive to this day in the mill cities of many New England villages.

Not at all a political statement, but rather an efficient delineation usually stated in French, all non-Francos were called by us "Americans" (Americains). We continued to call ourselves "Canadians" (Canadiens) until time gradually evolved the appellation (usually spoken in English now) to "French." Which I consider as egregiously false. I do not consider myself French; I am a proud American who happens to be a proud first-generation Franco-American.

Aware that we children would quickly learn English when we interacted with the outside, our parents required always and ever that we speak French "in the house." Although this edict felt like capital punishment at the time especially since I did not learn to speak English until I entered the first grade at age 6, today I can gratefully claim that my English and French have enriched my life, have facilitated travel all over the world. My French never impaired my English; it enhanced it.

As I consider my life at home as a child, I conclude it was a rather typical Franco upbringing. Were we poor? If so, we didn't know it. Enough to eat? Absolutely! And my mother was a master chef at transforming/combining random leftovers into delicious entrées enhanced by sauces, spices, and the like. We were required by our parents to eat evenly, i.e., each portion on our plate, along with bread and butter, given democratic attention.

True to most Franco families then, breakfast ("déjeuner"— contrary to *Petit Larousse*) was consumed immediately upon arising, lunch ("dîner") as close to noon sharp as possible depending on schedules, and supper ("souper") at a punctual 5:30 after we'd come home from school and my dad from work.

Well do I remember my dad's usual breakfast: juice, two eggs, thin slices of salt pork spread on toast. Hearty meals carried over from his youth and his days on my grandfather's farm, then metabolized in part, I believe, because of hard, physical labor.

Especially during the depression, on Sunday's my mom would cook a piece of meat (beef or pork favored) for our main meal which was usually eaten at noon. Complemented by potatoes and variegated veggies, my mom magically re-introduced each meal's remnant meat as a different species every "diner" until Thursday when it would mercifully and totally be consumed. How so? Whatever was left in the refrigerator was artistically transferred to a baking dish, strategically covered with pie crust and baked at 350 degrees until done! Observing meatless Friday's was infinitely more appealing to me (mackerel, haddock, or salmon with whipped potatoes and two vegetables) than the beans and franks Saturday fare. It seemed then we were served tons of vegetables, including onions. (Cannot enjoy, say, stringbeans today without first cooking them under onions and a generous piece of salt pork.) Delicious, usually warm, baked desserts that often included fruit, but little "still life" fruit. I remember promising myself as a child that I would someday grow a watermelon garden!

Supper (souper) too was a hardy meal that might be further categorized as a meeting. That's when my parents discussed their day and inquired about ours. The previous sentence is code for "what did you learn in school today?" These were not always festive Ozzie and Harriet events, believe me!

Although my mom sometimes catered to some of our finicky-ism, a favorite line of hers when we put up our nose at some planned or tabled dish was, "If it's good enough for your father who earns it, it's good enough for you."

As I wrote above, pork roast was a favorite. Sandwiches with pork butt meat saturated with delicious home-made ketchup were assembled between thick white bread slices the night before, and kept in the fridge until we fetched them the next morning for school or work. Exposed to room temperature all morning and lacking today's "kill dates," they were consumed with gusto at lunch. No one died.

Other frequent. non-Weight Watchers foods we enjoyed:

- **Pork pies (*tourtières*) especially around Thanksgiving and Christmas**
- **Hash (du hashie) diced potato, meat, onions in a brown sauce to use up leftovers**
- **Crêpes (especially on Fridays as lunch or dinner; with butter and/or syrup)**
- **Salt pork (*grillades the lard*) often sliced or diced and used as a butter substitute**
- **Pork spread (*cretons*) again around the holidays**
- **Blood pudding (*boudin*) sausage-like, pan-cooked in bacon and onion bits**

By the way, my dad lived to be 90, and my mom to 94!

In short, this whole business of the culinary can be summed up with the adjective "frugal." And "waste," after all these years, is still not part of that vocabulary. According to our parents, it wasn't that there were "children starving in China"; the reasoning given here was that no matter if we had eaten *boudin* (blood pudding) or *hashie* (hash) God had thus given us "our daily bread."

Most of our clothing were products of a collaborative feat: mom and I used to go to the Salvation Army Friday evening and carefully select used garments that she would later launder or have cleaned. Then she would unstitch and press them flat to yield yardage. Following this, my dad would then gingerly trace a pattern (some home-drawn, others either Simplicity or McCall's) a prospective piece of apparel on that cloth which my mother would later stitch together. And voilà! A coat or dress or even a brim hat... As I said, "frugal!"

My dad used to remark that there were only three food items they were required to outsource from the farm where he grew up: tea, flour, and sugar. Likewise, when it came to clothing in our own immediate family, the only purchased items were underwear, some stockings, and shoes.

In Juliana L'Heureux's column, "Les Franco-Americains," that appeared weekly in the *Portland Press Herald* (Maine), she quoted Connie Castille and her 25-minute documentary, "I Always Do My Collars First; a Film About Ironing."

It is a tribute to the pride French-Acadian women took in doing daily tasks. There was pristine pride and a meticulous attention to appearance and cleanliness. If so, most Franco-Americans relished giving it. Laundry day was usually Monday. Whites were soaked in a bluing solution to make them whiter. Collars, sleeve cuffs and other likely apparel were soaked in pots of cooked starch, either light or heavy, depending on the stiffness you wanted. Then the clothes were hung out to dry, even in the coldest weather, and that event had its own protocol too. Underwear gets hung on the inside lines where they are not obvious from the street. While still damp, clothes were brought in, rolled up in a pillow case, sprinkled with water (*humecter*) and placed into the ice box until it was time to iron.

Although we clung to our original Franco-American customs, it took the writing of this ethnic memoir to realize that my parents relocated from New Hampshire early in my youth and transplanted us to the west side of our town (as opposed to the more-Franco-populated east side), not at all considered a purely Franco-American conclave. Our so-called "middle class" neighborhood provided a rich milieu for growing up during those hormone-popping years. Due only to serendipity, we played baseball, hide and seek, even spin the bottle (now it can be told) with many harlequin ethnicities: Jews, Italians, Irish, Scotch, French, etc. If I screwed up, it was likely some knowing adult in that neighborhood cared enough about me to diplomatically inform my parents. (At least this is my reasoning today.)

One summer a town policeman who had stopped my teen brother earlier because of incredibly loud muffler action on his souped-up car appeared at our front door and asked my dad for his parental cooperation in taming the car's decibels — and my brother! I remember many situations when the neighborhood singularly or collectively sheltered us. And several sequential winters when an invincible pea jacket was shuttled around to whatever child fit it that year!

My parents absolutely reveled in hosting relatives, friends (theirs or ours). It was usually at our home where many holiday celebrations occurred that included lavish decorations, delish food (my mom, the Elsa Maxwell of our family who could also deftly morph into a comic via a hilarious monologue about life with father), beverages, quiz games, music sing-a-longs, and just plain jubilant fun! Likewise, many of our friends were heartily welcome to surround the piano in song while I accompanied them: "Peg Of My Heart," "Moonlight Bay," "Mockingbird Hill." When one of my brothers was cast in a high school play, full rehearsals were held at our house. Our friends loved to be with our parents, especially when they (my parents) would demonstrate the jitterbug or waltz dancing they were learning at the Arthur Murray Studio in the city!

Because they had never had the luxury of much formal education and they realized it was the "ticket," Francos highly valued learning. Here my mind often leaps back to the contractor who built our home and his telling me how pleadingly he begged his friend to teach him square root so he could calculate the pitch of a roof. Wow! A sign in my dad's office proudly proclaimed, "Success is one happy wife and five children with a sheepskin." (He was successful on all counts.) Mark Twain's adage about education was not just a staid bromide to them; every day they lived it: "If you think education is expensive, try ignorance." Yet their common sense, courage, and lifelong desire to learn imbued my parents with a confidence that seeped through the many arenas of their life, easing the void of what might be called "book learning."

One other value, barely a subset of education, was Music! Four of us were gifted with the ability to play the piano — "three by ear," but immediately after supper our piano stool — wherever in our home — was reserved seating for my dad who moseyed to it and serenaded us with both piano and voice as we cleared the table. At other times, my mom who favored more classical music, my brother or I would take turns at that same busy piano. Again, some of these songs were played/sung with considerable gusto in English, French or Latin (hymns).

Absent computers and television sets, most groups had sub-cultures, many church-related.

These were opportunities for socialization as well as for spiritual interaction. The Daughters of Isabella for women/ the Knights of Columbus for Men; le Club St. Jean Baptiste (furthering the Franco language and causes); Children of Mary for women only along with the more Anglo civic groups such as the Rotary, Elks, Lions, and others.

There was a great deal of respect accorded relationships: not only would we have never called our parents by their first names, we even prefaced the names of persons older than us according to their relationship identity to us: aunt Anita, uncle John, Mrs. Binette. Even though they were about the same age, my parents early on were prone to address their friends as either "Madame," "Mademoiselle,"

or "Monsieur."

Every single time we left the house bound for a date, my mom would wisely warn in French,

"Remember that for one moment of pleasure (*un petit moment de plaisir*), you can ruin your whole life."

Our parents were strict although retrospect informs me today that, in my case—being the only girl—there was truly a double-standard. Another Franco adage (or was it Confucius'): "It's the girl who carries the little package." Across my high school years, I was allowed to join school activities only two nights a week: once for Tuesday basketball practice and once for the Friday night hop. Not so my four brothers whose theme song might have been "Don't Fence Me In."

As I remember my parents, I am grateful for the discipline, common sense and courage they themselves modeled with everyday humility. My friends' parents typically had the same parental style. In a word, they unconsciously lived Herman Hesse's famous quote from *Siddhartha*: "I can think. I can wait. I can fast." Also, it was another time, prior to the 1960's, James Dean, and *Rebel Without A Cause*.

Today I understand that my parents' helicoptering behaviors (yea, B49 behaviors) were really what is called "tough love." (But even after all these years, that's one heck of an oxymoron to swallow!)

Joseph Côté
(Pépère)

Elmire Beauchesne
Côté
(Mémère)

**ôMom and Dad: Lauretta Côté Dutile
and Wilfred Dutile, Sr.
Honeymoon: November, 1933**

Lewiston, Maine
OFFICE OF THE CITY CLERK   N⁰   **523**
The Records of this Office show that
_____Wilfred Dutile_____ and
_____Laurette Cote_____
were married in Lewiston, Maine on __11-11-33__
Number of marriages:
Groom _____1st_____
Bride _____1st_____
_____ City Clerk

My parents' marriage certificate

1970: The author's immediate family: Wilfred Jr.,
David, Dad, Richard, Lorraine, Fernand, Mom

4

À L'hotel De Ville*

For forms of government let fools contest;
Whate'er is best administered is best

— ALEXANDER POPE

---

* At City Hall

~ À L'hotel De Ville ~

As a group and individually, Francos dearly wanted to become American citizens. Sanford Historian Gerard Lamontagne's research shows that becoming an American citizen was the highlight of a Franco's life.

At the age of 27 in 1937 my mother became a naturalized citizen. But not before she had expressed a great deal of apprehension. So scary, she pleaded, just the thought of studying "that book," being in a formal, public courtroom, and answering those questions regarding civic matters. (Maybe a good idea at this point in my story is to remember she was forced to leave school in the fifth grade.) It was only because of my dad's insistence — that if we ever went to war with her native country, Canada, she would be summarily extradited away from him and me — that she finally agreed to endure the "procedure."

Truth to tell, the citizenship test was not easy, especially administered in English, a second language for her and her siblings. I remember her telling me how nervous they all were just reviewing questions like:

1. What do the stripes on the flag symbolize?
2. How many changes or amendments are there to the Constitution?
3. Explain the legislative branch of our government.

But, aha, my mom's astonishing advantage was that she religiously read her newspaper every day!

Which prompts the question: how did these immigrants acquire/improve their reading comprehension?

No question: the greatest generation!

After considerable time and study, she and her siblings did all pass the dreaded examination and proudly became American citizens. Mom never forgot the gorgeous metaphor the judge pronounced that day explaining, "Your country of birth is like your parents while your new country, America, is like a spouse. When you marry, you don't disfavor your parents, and you should keep the same reverence for your country of birth."

Correction: one of my mother's siblings, Matante Maria, never did possess the temerity to apply for citizenship. But after living in this country for 50 years without a legal blemish (Aunt Maria didn't host too many keg parties), she passively received honorary American citizenship by way of a sublime letter and certificate from Washington, DC, signed by then-president of the United States, John Fitzgerald Kennedy!

A sign of the times: Today's societal arrangements as a result of education, dual careers in a family, and a simple sense of consideration for the Other have all but smudged family gender roles. Not so much in the past. My parents, like most then, held staunch theses about the government of our family which meant an automatic allocation of tasks: she it was who was responsible for keeping the home fires burning while he reigned at his place of business, a retail shoe store. Outdoors, raking, shoveling, etc. were moveable tasks among my dad, brothers, and me. Everyone in our family had a role, participated in its enterprise (if often reluctantly on the part of us kiddos), and this leads me to my next paragraph.

Never the suffragette, my mother also emphatically insisted that voting was not a woman's duty. *(C'est pas mon devoir!)* Again and over time, my dad contradicted her non-civic perception by claiming that, not only was this (voting) a gender-neutral obligation, it was a privilege to be able to do so. I don't think she would have ever voted without my dad's "homily," even leaving his work to fetch her, and transporting her to the polls.

Sanford historian Gilles Auger reports there was record voting in Sanford in 1936. In 1940, a new non-military "conscription law" emerged that compelled aliens to register. Of 890 who registered in our town, 800 were Francos.

I have several times heard from elders how absolutely mindful they were of the value of education, that once they graduated high school (likely as respected a credential then as a college degree today), their place in civic and social society so improved. How prescient they were! After proving themselves in school and in the marketplace, Francos have enjoyed more than proportionate representation at all levels of Maine government. I include in these our two recent candidates for Maine Governor, our 2nd District Representative, our City Mayor and Vice-mayor and many more on the national scene.

Initially Francos voted in the dominant Republican party, but lacked sufficient representation on my hometown Sanford's Board of Selectmen (they believed). In 1910 a small group of the frustrated held a Democratic rally, and the subsequent shift in party affiliation placed Sanford in the Democratic ranks where it remains. Today in Maine, 39% of Franco voters are Democrats; 22% Republicans; and 38% not affiliated with either party. My parents were staunch Democrats, and I was 40 years old before I learned that Hoover's first name was not "maudit" – English translation: "damn!"

We are sometimes perversely called "frogs," and I have no idea the genesis of that. As comic acknowledgement, the Franco-American students at the University of Maine in Orono publish a student newspaper titled *THE FAROG* (Franco-American Research and Opportunity Group). By the way, their telephone number is (207) 581-FROG.

There was/is still? considerable prejudice though about us Franco immigrants. "Your French is not Parisian French," we hear, knowing that their English is not London English. So there! Plenty of reason why some Francos deny their heritage and change their last name from Boulanger to Baker, from Poisson to Fisher, etc.

As a university administrator, I sometimes registered students from the very Franco northern part of Maine whose English was often tenuous. Sensing their verbal struggle, I would casually, gently slip to French, but they would have none of it. Again, the yearning for assimilation.

My parents, on the other hand, believed there was more prejudice about being Catholic than about being of French extraction. The jury is still out about that conclusion.

Maine has the greatest proportion (5.28%) of French-speaking people at home — more than has any other American State. We are second only to New Hampshire in the percentage of Franco-Americans who reside in our State.

A local rumor has it that one of our nuns decided to conduct a survey about her first-graders. Having asked them to put their head down on their desk, she asked, "Please raise your hand if you have a mémère." Apparently, many hands went up.

We kept such a low profile that it was only in 1977 that Maine recognized Franco-Americans as an ethnic group, even though we had been here for scores of years. A UMO professor, Susan Pinette, agrees that, even though 23% of our population is Franco-American, that fact is hardly seen in Maine demographics. Because Maine is so "white," we continuously strive for diversity. It can be argued that, at least among Caucasians, 23% of us provide that ethnic alternative.

It is truly what Dyke Hendrickson's book, *Quiet Presence*, clearly illustrates. His sister book, "*Franco-Americans of Maine*," Dyke makes the following claim:

> Nearly one-third of Maine residents have French blood and are known as Franco-Americans. Many trace their heritage to French Canadian families who came south from Quebec in the late 19th and early 20th centuries to work in the mills of growing communities such as Auburn, Augusta, Biddeford, Brunswick, Lewiston, Saco, Sanford, Westbrook, Winslow, and Waterville. Other Franco-Americans, known as Acadians, have rural roots in the St. John Valley in northernmost Maine.

It cannot be said that we Francos "lost" our culture or language even though both today are eclipsed primarily because of time and new generations. Admittedly, we eagerly, if slowly, forfeited our traditions over the arc of the years to share The American Dream which included the rich culture America offered, the opportunity to be gainfully and predictably employed, and the fabulous permutations resulting from these two. In other words, through assimilation, these Original Dreamers richly gained both standard of living and quality of life—their dreams realized. A cherished barter and a most happy outcome although sometimes some of us seniors share Tevye's yearning for "*Tradition*!"

5

À L'ouvrage*

*The progress of human society consists...in...
the better and better apportioning of wages to work.*

— THOMAS CARLYLE

---

* At the workplace

~ À L'ouvrage ~

MY DAD, OVER the several years of his employment life, worked in a Lewiston bleachery tracing patterns on dyed or bleached cloth ("In the bleaching process the use of chloride of lime was replaced by sodium hypochlorite made by bubbling chlorine gas into an alkaline sodium solution. In turn, the three day bleaching process gave way to a one day continuous peroxide process." – *Lewiston Evening Journal*, March 3, 1975) — yikes!, he hung wallpaper and painted (@ $.25 per hour), was a representative of the Internal Revenue Service ("If you can't beat 'em, join em") until he braved the risk of opening a what-was-then one of the first self-serve grocery stores in New Hampshire (IGA) and, finally, established a retail shoe store in Maine.

Contrary to most Quebec immigrants, my mom never worked in the textile mills. Rather, she had proudly learned to be a fancy stitcher in the shoe shops of Lewiston and Auburn. This job title was aggrandized as a "trade," which is why her salary usually exceeded my dad's during the early days of their marriage. I remember her and my dad home at night gleefully calculating the cases of shoes she had stitched that day and rejoicing at the sorely-needed dollars this would mean on payday. As was the possibility for most manufacturing employees, the companies offered great motivators to work hard, fast, and well. One of these was so-called "piece work" (after certain quotas had been met) when the wage was calculated according to production volume as opposed to a baser, consistent hourly rate.

About textile jobs, folklore claims believably that men were assigned the heavy work. One example would be the setting up, operating, or tending machines that wound or twisted textiles; or drawing out and combining sliver such as wool, hemp, or synthetic fibers. In contrast, some women might hustle at a function called "burling," a finishing process to improve the appearance of the unbleached cloth by removing knots, loose threads, etc. Also, it was the women who usually mended and folded cloth.

My mom's vocational arena, the shoe shop, had parallel protocols: women sewed the top of a shoe while men addressed the bottom or sole. Of course, fewer women worked in those times.

Like the English Protestants whose work ethic was assessed to be sterling, Francos too enjoyed a reputation that was superb about their respective occupations. They were quick, agile, and eager to learn since, from day one, their humble calculus clearly illustrated the correlation between education and reward. My grandfather could not even sign his name, but being the focused employee he was, he was allowed a stencil and a paintbrush with which he could brand an "X" identifying his work. Neither my parents or I have any idea why their mother (my grandmothers) were able to understand and read the French newspapers to their illiterate husbands in the evening.

Because the Roman Catholic Church (to which most Francos belonged) forbade (still forbids) birth control, these immigrants bore many children. To this day when one is touring mill cities like Lewiston, this thesis is rumored and attested to by the vision of old, cavernous three-story apartment buildings that often each sheltered some 45 or more tenants.

There was relatively little public welfare to speak of even during those depression years due to a lack of government resources and since so stigmatized could one be by the denunciation and idiom that s/he was "on the town." A family in need could likely get assistance at their local town/city hall, receiving food staples such as lentils, flour, and sugar. It was certainly an employer's market as explained in the following quote by Linda Levine, Specialist in Labor Economics, comparing the Great Depression to the recent 2009 Recession:

In 1933, at the depth of the Depression, one in four workers was unemployed. In contrast, the unemployment rate had risen to 9.4% by May 2009. The number of jobs on nonfarm payrolls fell 24.3% between 1929 and 1933. Thus far during the current [2009] recession, firms have cut nonfarm employment by

4.3%. The first 17 months of the ongoing recession compare favorably with the first two years of the Depression as well.

In addition to the greater magnitude of unemployment and job loss during the early 1930s as compared with today, the implications of being unemployed have changed much in the intervening years. One reason for the altered situation facing today's unemployed is the increased prevalence of families in which both spouses work. Another is the deeper drop in earnings and hours worked that occurred during the Depression. And, the social safety net that is now available to displaced workers and their families did not exist before the onset of the Great Depression.

If a child (usually a male) was fortunate enough to be allowed to stay in school through the eighth grade, s/he was expected to immediately get a job and help support the family. If that child was a female, she would not likely be allowed the advantage of eight grades of schooling because the culture absolutely valued males over females. Yes, that paycheck — except for necessities like transportation to and from work — was automatically forfeited to the household finances. But, once one became engaged to be married, s/he was allowed to keep the earnings in order to prepare financially for the future. And it was just about this time in their lives that engaged females would start stocking a cedar chest with sundry sheets, towels, blankets, and other items that constituted a dowry (property or money brought by a bride to her husband on their marriage).

Some manufacturing employees initially worked six days a week, twelve hours a day from 6:00 am to 6:00 pm, then 5.5 days, then finally 5. There was no such entity as OSHA, and the fumes alone in some of those shoe and textile shops were so sensuously acrid until, after some time, one had staggeringly grown immune to them. Once the summer's heat invaded the spacious workrooms, it was seldom alleviated by ventilation from open windows until the weather outside turned truly frigid. Of course, there was no sick, annual, or bereavement leave; no medical insurance. Textile mill workers' exposure to asbestos was largely the result of direct handling of asbestos that was used to produce textiles. Exposure to airborne asbestos fibers and asbestos-containing insulation around machinery was a concern for all workers in the mill, whether handled palpably or not. Before strict regulations on the use of asbestos were implemented, the process of converting asbestos into usable fabric was one that involved many different workers and locations throughout the mill. Even though some of that work was endured under primitive conditions (highly repetitive, physical, unhealthful), it was usually considered an improvement over what their past lives had suffered. Any possible overtime called "time and a half" (time after the regular workweek) was grabbed!

In 1900 prevailing wages were $390 per year which would be about $10,000 in today's dollars. The point is exactly the one my dad used to make, "Bread was a dime, but no one had a nickel." Surely, today there is much more discretionary income in the case of most of us folks.

If you were a doctor, you made house calls equipped with that little black satchel you see in movies of the past.

If you were a grocer, you likely penciled and calculated your customer's purchases on a brown paper bag and extended credit, recording it by transmitting the total (again with a pencil) on a simple cardstock sheet inscribed with his name. Your customer would likely square up with you on Friday, the most common payday.

When you consider all of the benefits a job and a predictable paycheck represented, it is no wonder that Francos regaled in their new surroundings.

If Franco's work ethic was exemplary, as a general statement, they were clearly rewarded, respected, and appreciated. In some instances, even lower-cost or new housing came into play from generous managers who were aware that happy employees made for good business. Meanwhile most Francos became ever so encouraged about their standard of living and quality of life since they, with time, ascended the yellow brick road to the Middle Class!

6

À L'église*

*I like the silent church before the service begins,
better than any preaching.*

— RALPH WALDO EMERSON

---

* At church

~ À L'église ~

Y OU LIKELY KNOW that most Franco-Americans' lives were so entwined with the Roman Catholic Church that where one left off and the other began truly defines the word "smudge."

Just as every village featured a town square at its very center, so it was that Franco communities of any size included at least one place of worship. In fact, their generous tendency to support the construction of churches (whose more expensive, elaborate architecture arguably eclipsed the comely simplicity of Protestant churches) is both understandable, if disputable.

One stark example of their value system in this spiritual realm of their lives is the Basilica of Sts. Peter and Paul in Lewiston, ME. Actually built during the darkest years of the Depression although it had been planned for three decades and funds for it slowly set aside, it was not until the dark times during the 1930s that the parishioners made the final push to build it, holding every community event possible to raise money. In this parish of shoe-factory and textile-mill workers, there were no great benefactors available. And so the $800,000 ($11,358,611 in 2017 dollars) it took to build this cathedral-size church was raised literally nickel by nickel, dime by dime. And that amazing cost did not include many of its requisite ecclesiastical *accoutrements*, small or large, such as the three organs in the gallery, sanctuary, and lower church, the gold chalices, patens, candlesticks and other altar accessories, artwork, baroque woodwork, columns. This is not to conclude that all parishioners agreed with this prodigality, but simply that most did. Perhaps the European churches with their extravagant types of architecture inspired them to believe that such excess commensurately bespoke fervor. But whether small or large, all Catholic churches held and still hold to the same common denominator standards of liturgy, providing the comfort — spiritual and otherwise — of universality wherever one journeys.

Somewhat contrary to today's convention and absolutely financially strategic, the parishes were territorial insofar as which congregants belonged to which parish. Talk about ecclesiastical administration! In my own hometown, the line of demarcation even ran down one single street (Brook) with church members living on the left mandated to worship at the east-side church, Holy Family, while those whose homes were situated on the right side of that same street were claimed as west-side parishioners at St. Ignatius. Further, there was the "French church," "the Irish church," and possibly the Eastern Rite of the Catholic Church. And notwithstanding, it is intriguing to note that congregants actually self-identified (hence, explaining both the geographic location of their home and place of worship) by actually disclosing, with pride, to which parish they belonged. Identity politics no less.

Full disclosure: stuff we were not allowed to do: visit a non-Catholic church, read *The Bible*, participate in a Protestant church ceremony. And, of course, we were taught that we were the only ones going to heaven. This latter conviction was soundly predicated on the thesis that ours was the one, true faith.

Although my parents were staunch Roman Catholics who religiously adhered to the tenets of their faith (like most Catholic families, a crucifix hung on one of the walls in our home), in retrospect I believe their words and actions well-substantiated they were open to other views or doctrines. "Any 'kind' of religion makes people better," I often heard my mom say. They walked the talk and were incredibly generous to anyone in need. As example, my dad, a retail shoe man, gifted the reputed-poor people of a nearby town with hundreds of pairs of shoes every year.

The liturgical year went something like this (deep breath, please):

- Thanksgiving, of course, was a day of giving thanks. More than that, it was the beginning of the holiday season for us (les fêtes – the feasts from that date to Epiphany on January 6). That's also when the pork pies (tourtières) and pork spread (cretons) started to show up on our kitchen/dining room table;
- Four weeks before Christmas was/is called "Advent." This is still considered a penitential time when priests

don purple priestly vestments. The third Sunday of Advent is called "Gaudete (Rejoice) Sunday" when rose vestments are worn to symbolize hope in a season of darkness. The *Introit* of the Mass beckons, "Rejoice in the Lord always; again I say, rejoice. Let your forbearance be known to all, for the Lord is near at hand; have no anxiety about anything, but in all things, by prayer and supplication, with thanksgiving, let your requests be known to God. Lord, you have blessed your land; you have turned away the captivity of Jacob." Philippians 4:4–6; Psalm 85 (84):1;

- Christmas finally arrived! We called it "Noël." This comes from the French phrase "les bonnes nouvelles" which means "the good news" and refers to the gospel. Although Christmas decorations had abounded everywhere else, as is the protocol now in the Church, Christmas day was/is the very first time in the entire season when the church was so-decorated. Of course, every church and French home at Christmastime displayed a Nativity scene or crèche, which served as the focus for the Christmas celebration. Said crèche was always peopled with little clay figures called santons or "little saints." The usual Holy Family, shepherds, and three Magi graced the humble commemorative stable scene where Christ was simulated to have been born. Unlikely though it was/is in Bethlehem in December, we shower the crèche with abundant snow. Also, we value-impregnate Jesus (a Jew) and two Magi as Caucasians, allowing for Balthazar as a young man from Yemen, very often and increasingly black-skinned, presenting myrrh. Montesquieu: "If triangles worshipped God, he would have three sides;"

- Midnight mass, Christmas eve, in many parishes, was an elegant event that actually required reservations. Many women wore corsages and formal gowns while it is true that even some men were also formally dressed. At 11:55 pm a soulful tenor would intone the dramatic "Minuit, Chrétiens" (Midnight, Christians) which most know as "O, Holy Night." Editorial comment: nowhere, anywhere in the written word does the beauty of the French language more transpire than in this lyric. Impossible to explain all of the poetic, exotic idioms therein. Gorgeous liturgy prevailed throughout the occasion, varied pomp and circumstance, much of it respectfully akin to pre-Vatican II liturgy. The French traditions of Christmas continue to this day to be an integral part of celebrating the birth of Jesus. They consist of many favorite customs such as the Christmas tree, the chocolate bûche (log), the Père Noël (Santa Claus) and the great after-Mass Christmas Eve dinner we call the "reveillon" (the awakening);

- Yes, midnight Mass was followed with a lavish, rich, festive meal, *reveillon*! Oh, those pork pies and other culinary delights that landed in one's stomach not unlike an anvil. Usually celebrated with music, folklore, and adult beverages after which, around 3:00

am, it was high time for parents to rush home, get a few hours sleep before their children would rise and pant for Père Noël's goodies;

- New Year's Day too was a "holy day of obligation" (that's Latin for compulsory Mass) and a holiday when — amongst other more festive functions — one would kneel and seek a blessing for the coming year from the oldest male relative who lived in the immediate area. Yep; gender-tilted!

- As ever, January 6th, Epiphany, recalled the star that guided the wise men to Christ as well as the three gifts they gave to Jesus: gold, frankincense, or myrrh. In turn small gifts were exchanged among close family members in remembrance of that event;

- Ho, February 3: gotta get that throat blessed, remembering that Saint Blaise, the bishop of Sebaste in Armenia during the fourth century, was reputed to have miraculously cured a little boy who nearly died because of a fishbone in his throat. Onward to Mass (again!) that included a St. Blaise blessing — two candles held in a crossed position that touched both sides of the throat. At the same time the following prayer was/is said: "May Almighty God at the intercession of St. Blaise, Bishop and Martyr, preserve you from infections of the throat and from all other afflictions."

- St. Valentine's Day, St. Patrick's Day were/are fervently celebrated much the way the rest of the country did/does! Cue the music!;

- Well, before you could blink an eyelash, Mardi Gras (the day before the penitential season of Lent) dawned. Usually celebrated about mid-February — late winter and early spring as the maple syrup harvest begins and the snow is still on the ground. Home-made troughs were filled with clean (white) snow over which was poured boiled and reduced maple syrup, chilling it to a taffy-like consistency. The taffy was then rolled up on wooden sticks and eaten. Luscious, if not recommended by the American Dental Association!

- Ash Wednesday presented the opportunity for a new fashion statement — receiving ashes on our forehead. While some priests' artwork looked like calligraphy around the bangs area of the face, other priests scribed a more muted symbol. All priests reminded us: "Remember that thou are dust and to dust you wilt become." And while some parishioners preferred to conserve this inspiration on their foreheads at work or at play throughout the day, others were seen peering in their car mirror as they scrubbed the evidence driving out of the church parking lot;

- The forty long days of Lent had begun. Priests were attired in penitential purple vestments, resolutions for us kiddos usually involved giving up candy and were the subject of much debate as to whether or not Sunday was a "legal" respite from the resolve, the Sacrament of Marriage absolutely forbidden, the Rosary said in church Wednesday afternoons, the

Way of the Cross Friday afternoons with the *Sancta Mater Istud Agas* hymn sung at every one of the 14 stations.

- Replicating Advent a bit, *Laetare Sunday*, so-called from the Introit at Mass, "Laetare Jerusalem" ("Rejoice, O Jerusalem"), from Isaiah 66:10, denoted the fourth Sunday of the season of Lent when the hopeful-rose priestly vestments again replaced the despondent purple;

- Palm Sunday commemorated Christ's triumphal entry into Jerusalem! Palms were distributed with jubilant music analogous to Andrew Lloyd Webber's "Hosanna Hey Sanna Sanna Sanna Hosanna Hey Sanna Hosanna…" While most lay persons later respectfully manipulated or circled their palms around their home crucifixes, artistic or clerical persons wove them into intricately beautiful artifacts;

- Finally, Lent mercifully culminated into long prayers and ceremonies at Mass Holy Thursday, Good Friday, Holy Saturday, and eureka! Easter Sunday! But not before we had made the compulsory Easter Duties, that is, gone to Confession if we had not already fulfilled that obligation during the past year. The lines were interminable, and it was often the case that penitents would drop in, visually assess the length of the confessional line, exit, and return for another peek until a do-able wait was assured;

- As extension of that thought, as young children even, we were taught long prayers which we memorized by rote. And if you were serendipitously subject to "The Litany of The Saints" as part of a given church ceremony, you soon discovered as you discretely petitioned each saint to pray for you, that their number seemed to far exceed that of the present church attendees!

- Easter Sunday was everything Irving Berlin wrote about, and then some: certainly an Easter bonnet for women, dyed shoes and purse, gorgeous and festive liturgy and music in celebration of Christ's rising from the dead. All this reflective of the Church's thesis about Easter — the most important holy day in the liturgical year;

- May, devoted to the Blessed Mother, presented another opportunity for family prayer. In this case, rosary beads said kneeling somewhere in the home (usually "the parlor") led by a member of the household (usually the mom). Should a visitor knock at the door, my own mother would motion him forth and gently summon him to join the family in prayer;

- While Bastille day, July 14th, relates to France, Franco-Americans identified more with St. Jean Baptiste's feast day, a remnant from their former country, Canada: Saint-Jean-Baptiste Day (French: *Fête de la Saint-Jean-Baptiste*), officially known in Quebec as La fête nationale, (English: National Holiday) is a holiday celebrated annually on June 24, the feast day of the Nativity of St. John the Baptist. June 24 is also celebrated as a festival of French Canadian culture in other Canadian provinces and the United States;

- Besides all of the above, there were many holy days during the liturgical year — some "holy days of obligation" — when attending Mass, as I said, was compulsory;

- Because of the bilingual aspect of our towns/cities, some homilies were often delivered in English and then totally translated in French. Mon Dieu!

- "Sunday clothes" were dramatically different, "dressier" than weekday clothes. Of course, women wore hats to church as had dictated Paul, and we often proudly stayed "Sunday-dressed" all day;

- At the First Holy Communion Mass, girls were given shiny white prayer books while boys received black ones. Later, we were gifted a Missal that featured Latin on the left pages and English or French on the right-hand ones. This was a *sine qua non* requisite at all church ceremonies. Mercifully, the Church now affords us a soft cover version of same.

- Since we were required to fast from midnight the eve before until we actually received Holy Communion the next morning, there was absolutely nothing ingested in between those two events. And if it was snowing on the way to church, you made certain not to have any of that snow fall on your tongue lest you inadvertently break your fast.

- Funerals (*Requiem* Masses) because of their then-ultra-negative aspects emphatically contradicted the Christian tenet of the blessed next life. Following the casket, as pallbearers escorted it down the middle aisle, was a priest (if your stipend was generous enough, three priests — deacon, sub-deacon) clad in a heavy "dark black" chasuble while a choir musically threatened (*fortissimo*) the *Dies Irae*: This poem describes the day of judgment, the last trumpet summoning souls before the throne of God, where the saved will be delivered and the unsaved cast into eternal flames. Thankfully, today's Mass for the Dead combines the hopeful aura of white vestments along with corresponding hymns;

- Venial sin: mortal sin? Well, in order to commit a mortal sin, there were more clauses involved (catechism facts: you have to know what you're doing, it must be pre-meditated, you must want to do it, etc., etc.) than are part and parcel of the Treaty of Versailles. My most frequent sin in my youth, as I recall, was "hitting my brother." To this day, since this act was never the result of pre-meditation and he has no scars, I conclude that sin was venial, if perhaps undeserved...

- Fortunately and eventually too, the Church got in *sinc* with Martin Luther (only 600 years later) and has practically aborted the concept of indulgences as we understood them. Recall that an indulgence is a remission before God of the temporal punishment due to sins. And one of my great consolations as a sinner-child regarding the guilt of hitting my brother (my most frequent confession) or teasing him to disobey by peeing outside was the promise that reciting "Jesus, Mary, and Joseph" ransomed me seven whole years from hell every time I said it. Believe me, that was one of my most common prayers!

- The Church presented us with a value system that included, of course, The Ten Commandments, Seven Sacraments, Legion of Decency Lists that graded the appropriateness of movies for its members, Commandments of the Church (tithing, fasting, attending Mass, etc., examples of virtues and, yes, sinfulness!).

- The liturgical year for Franco-Americans was very much part of their DNA and the perfect complement to the long prayers learned by rote at an early age along with that Roman Catholic best seller, *The Baltimore Catechism.* Is there a parochial school alumnus who doesn't remember from way back in the first grade:

 "Who made you?"

 "God made me."

 "Why did God make you?"

"God made me to know him, love him and serve him in this world, and to be happy with him forever in the next."

Eighty-three years later, it may or may not surprise you to learn that I am incredibly grateful for the intimate interaction my family sustained because of the Church. Like every other organization it had and has its warts, but no other could have so profoundly provided the embellishing texture of a moral compass in our developing lives, a spiritual ideal of altruism and compassion, a thoughtful sequence of seasons that lighted the way.

Indeed, amazing grace!

In summary, again, it was an Old-World upbringing that prepared us for the hope of Another World.

7

À L'école*

*Then rising with Aurora's light
The Muse invoked, sit down to write;
Blot out, correct, insert, refine,
Enlarge, diminish, interline.*

— JONATHAN SWIFT

---

* At school

~ À L'école ~

School days, school days
Good old golden rule days
Readin' and writin' and 'rithmetic
Taught to the tune of a hickory stick

ALTHOUGH THERE HAS ever been much banter across the ages about authoritarian nuns looming over bewildered youngsters, armed with rulers intended for rapping students' knuckles in order to instill correct behavior or academics, none of these scenarios punctuated my twelve years at Catholic schools. And that includes "hickory sticks."

Because of Francos' strong belief in Catholic education, requiring them to eke out of their meager salaries the costs of both municipal taxes and parochial school tuition, a small town like ours (Sanford, Maine, population in the early 20th Century about 17,000) encompassed three elementary schools (built 1895, 1916, and 1923) and a commercial two-year high school (1939) which later evolved into a full four-year high school (1941). Repeatedly stressed over and over again, using their bully pulpit, our priests promulgated the moral responsibility of parents enrolling children in Catholic schools. While the Ursuline Order of Nuns taught all of the girls' classes in my high school; those of the boys were led by The Brothers of Christian Education.

Research demonstrates that Sanford parochial school enrollments peaked in the mid-nineteen-forties at which time they totalled 1,430 students led by a mere 37 faculty members. Let me do the math for you: each class averaged 39 students. Of course, these schools took the burden off the public school system and the town budget. Today, without factoring in classroom or mandated support services, a simple division operation reads as follows: the dividend of 1,430 students, the divisor of 30 students per classroom, yields the quotient or need for 48 classrooms staffed by 48 classroom teachers. Not to mention support staff. Yowza!

My parents were certain adherents of that parochial school system; their strong belief in education in general was likely mostly spawned by the fact that they had been allowed so little of it. In their paucity of academe, they were certainly not alone.

Even though I can't remember any stigmata episodes with rulers, I do clearly remember the quasi-militaristic behavior that was expected of us. The following should give you a good idea of the strong academic and behavioral aspects of attending Catholic school then:

1. We raised our hand to speak and stood (to speak) only after having been recognized by the teacher;

2. No student was taught to cook, drive, or make love. We couldn't even chew gum;

3. Speaking of cursive, the nuns tutored us in the Palmer Writing method whereby we learned to write symmetrically against a background of slanted vertical strokes or impeccably concentric circles;

4. Some years, all of our morning classes were taught in French while English prevailed in the afternoon;

5. One memorable outgrowth of parochial school education was the "buying of pagan babies." For the uninitiated, let me explain: a small cardboard box was exhibited to the class by the nun with a plea that any extra money we had should be deposited in said box to redeem (snatch from Limbo) babies born to an irreligious family. Once the contents of that box equaled $5, the class would name the baby. The baptismal name had to be the name of a saint. A couple of times we tried to name that babe "Skippy."

6. Our stark buildings usually featured bathrooms on just one floor. Except for emergencies, we peed only mid-morning or mid-afternoon when recess occurred;

7. While today's high schools often emulate country clubs — complete with mini town halls at the center of their beings and student services offices decorated in muted pastels surrounding same — our high school's architectural scheme featured a dank atmosphere: drab walls, varnished desks screwed to the

floor, bare and rackety floorboards, devoted nuns in black habits, and a crucifix on a student-visible wall. Our high school floor was always fiercely demarcated by gender — except, in the case, understandably, of a chemistry lab that was necessarily and frugally shared by all! My recollection is that although accessible to both genders, it was strategically and precisely located smack at the demarcation line;

8. There was no cafeteria; we walked home (.7 of a mile) and back for lunch. Guidance consisted of Sister Mary Carmelita imploring us, "Have the courage of your convictions." Instead of an electronic buzzer denoting discrete class periods; one student was charged with the honor of ringing a small bell between classes. There were 49 students and one nun in my freshman class;

9. Because of lack of resources, the science curriculum was weak while the humanities offerings such as history, languages, and religion soared. We were taught Ursuline etiquette, most evident in our Glee Club activities when we competed (white skirts, navy blue jackets with gold seal, white gloves, navy crew cap) in the Western Maine Music Festival and — many years — came in first;

10. In my senior year of high school, some of us with a propensity for the classics were allowed to enroll in an accelerated French literature course. (As a former college administrator, I look back on that high school course as one equal to or exceeding college-level

offerings.) Since the high school could afford only one book, every day the nun/teacher would read to us aloud from that book of French classics during the entire semester. The experience was rich on so many levels because of authors like Flaubert, Madame de Sevigny, La Rochefaucauld, LaFontaine, Jean Jacques Rousseau, Proust, *et le reste*...;

11. Required daily dress for us girls was a navy blue jumper (with inverted pleats) on which at the left breast was the embossed gold seal of the school. The evolving color of those jumpers (from blue to a shiny, almost green hue by the senior year) was a correlative of the number of times they had been pressed. A white blouse, Peter Pan collar, if you please, provided cover and color. Finally, we wore regulation black shoes, some patent leather, even though it was never rumored hereabouts that these sinfully reflected "up;"

12. Competitive sports included boys' football, baseball and basketball for boys and girls. Boys sports (class C) were the object of much clamor and ink since they competed regionally with other teams. Alas, our girls' basketball team was dramatically more muted. The team owned just one ball (honest!), was coached by a volunteer college student, and played only one game annually with her college team. Talk about conflict of interest. Except that she was an amazing person with a good heart. Spoiler alert: none of us ever qualified for the Olympics;

13. Extracurricular activities at our small high school included Student Council, National Honor Society, Key Club, Gold and Blue Newspaper, Ursuline Order Awards, May Queen festivals, sodality, and other enriching experiences.

It was rumored and soundly substantiated that our school held to a very strong sense of academics and discipline. Comically expressed: that Catholic school children practiced a more elaborate system of behavior than is required of the Chief of Protocol at the Court of St. James. In retrospect, I can conclude that the school was poor, but there was no poverty of spirit. What we lacked in financial resources, we made up for in spirit, drive, and pride. This intriguing inversion is hardly an anomaly insofar as small organizations are concerned.

Our parents and faculty worked hand-in-hand and presented many motivational tools to encourage that level of excellence: one of them was fear. If you did misbehave in school and your parents found out, there was no quibbling about the question of innocence. You were automatically also admonished/punished at home. A parent may have gone behind the scenes to negotiate with the nun or brother, but as far as the student was concerned, that was all classified information! In other words, "The glove always fit so they didn't acquit."

In 1987, good friend Gary Sullivan (God rest his soul) and I co-hosted (with a rep from every class from 1941 to 1987) a parochial school reunion for all alumni. The turnout was so positive, over 1,200 attendees, we were forced to move the evening's festivities from our small parochial school gymnasium to the Holiday Inn in Portland, Maine.

Gary and I composed a script about the adventure of having attended parochial school which we recited piecemeal between the various acts each graduating class had produced. Here are excerpts:

Lorraine: You have to agree with me, Gary, that going to parochial school was a very distinctive experience.

Gary: Remember those nuns and THE ruler? I know a nun who used to carry her ruler in a shoulder holster, always ready for action. "Sister Mary Adolph," we called her. And boy, did some of us deserve it! We would have driven Francis of Assissi to crack/cocaine. You always knew who the Protestants were though; they could meet a nun head-on and never flinch. Yes, it was in Sanford, Maine that we all came of age, the town that had just one Yellow Page.

Lorraine: And how about that Baltimore Catechism, Gary?

Gary: Right. Remember that question about why Catholic schoolchildren are so healthy?

Lorraine: Yes; Catholic schoolchildren are unusually healthy because of the years of accumulation of Vick's Vaporub on their scapulas. (A cloth "medal" worn around the neck imploring the need to call a priest in the case of an accident.) How about another one of those catechism questions: Are Catholic children prepared for martyrdom?

Gary: Oh, that one's easy to remember. Catholic schoolchildren ARE prepared for martyrdom and would be HAPPY to stand up for their faith. Touché. And back to you to make sure if you remember the answer to this catechism question: Who is likely to ask a Catholic schoolchild to renounce his faith?

<u>Lorraine:</u> The Communists [alluding to the 50s] are likely to ask a Catholic schoolchild to renounce his faith because they are committed to defiling the souls of Catholic schoolchildren.

Alas, today only a small staff that includes two nuns among a half-dozen lay teachers and one building, a regional elementary school, replace the caring, fervent nuns and the several fabulous edifices that once sheltered and educated thousands of students. Countless alumni whose preparation there prefaced extraordinary success in many walks of life. The present school welcomes all faith communities and enrolls approximately 15% non-Catholics.

And so it went throughout our Catholic high school years: endless epiphanies of swirling marvels, prerogatives of youth — dreaded rank cards, Elvis Presley, whispers that so and so liked so and so, often- raging hormones, *Tantum Ergo Sacramentum*, elementary propositions/barter with the deity about hoped-for miracles, and — in general — à la Shakespeare, "such stuff that dreams are made on."

I am pleased to report that, of a graduating class of 24 women, approximately 10 of us (early octogenerians) meet for lunch the first Wednesday of every month, testimony to the seeds of faith, academic pride, and strong ties tenderly sown many years ago, yet cherished to this day.

8

Dad

The child that is not clean and neat,
With lots of toys and things to eat,
He is a naughty child, I'm sure —
Or else his dear papa is poor.

— ROBERT LOUIS STEVENSON

~ Dad ~

MY FIRST RECOLLECTION of him is of a non-winter day long ago; yesterday's spread-out newspaper protected the cold, massive kitchen stove's ebony top. A fanatic for education, his long fingers grazed short words there — contrapuntal to his phonetic reading lesson to me, the first grader.

Black and white. Black and white. The stove, the newspaper, his will and allegiance to principle. Self-discipline, as discrete and intense as Gregorian chant notes, spanned the score of his life.

He was at once patriarch, lover, superman, counselor, joker, dad, and other names. Like "anomaly." Once I witnessed a most lucrative business deal conducted between a client sitting at our family kitchen table and "him" wiping the dinner dishes for my mom.

I was forty before I realized he could be afraid.

His was a magnificent obsession with perfection. Quality was never negotiable. Because, "If it's worth doing, it's worth doing well." On the other hand, he could sometimes understand why "shortcuts" from school can cause a young-ster to arrive home late for dinner.

Call him also "methodical." He knew, I am certain, ex-actly how many seconds it should take to button a shirt or how many steps there were from our kitchen where he sliced the meat micrometrically to, say, his bedroom where he did not so much arrange as align his bedclothes. Seldom one for change, there was no soap like Camay, no toothpaste like Colgate, and no deodorant like Mum. He was indeed a saint, and we all put up with him!

It is difficult to paint him on this piece of paper. For, if he could be a scientist, so could he be a poet. Lover of surprises, birthdays and Christmases were always first-class feasts, high holidays prefaced by much anticipation and whis-pering, culminating into a swirling, rushing, and ha! ha! of the colors of his life. I recall as well sparkling, brilliant Necco circles of Sunday afternoon car rides through country woods he regarded as majestic! White, and ever whiter, birches were his favorite, and he would point them out as we rode, with exclamation and childlike simplicity. Three of us (then) in the back seat would always begin by fighting "for a side." We would usually sing on the way home: French, Latin, and English songs. And no one dared tell dad his harmony was too loud. Except my mom.

Though little formally educated, his philosophical out-look is perhaps best expressed by Kipling's "If" and Thomas' "Do Not Go Gentle." When we confessed dread for some impending challenge, he would facially and vocally feign astonishment and incredulously exhort, "What? Just make sure you prepare yourself, go in there with your head held high, and you'll do better than anyone else there." Even though his prophesies were sometimes unfulfilled concerning our level of excellence, his inspiration was unmistakable. He also taught us how to lose. If it was absolutely necessary to do so.

As I think of him many years hence, I am grateful less for the physical things he so well provided than for the spiritual gifts he instilled such as responsibility, courage, and inner strength. As the shadows of my own life enter and leave my space, as surely they must, his legacy provides light.

Because my dad lived, the world is better.

I love you, dad.

(1965)

9

Mom

So for the mother's sake the child was dear,
And dearer was the mother for the child.

— SAMUEL TAYLOR COLERIDGE

~ Mom ~

MY MOTHER'S LIFE is like a poem: not necessarily rhyming, but open-hearted, textured, spiritual, clarifying.

Originally a peasant immigrant from Canada who was forced to leave school in the fifth grade for lack of shoes, she speaks fluently in two languages of statesmen, actors, and Miss Manners.

My first recollection of her is in a movie theatre: Judy Garland, "The Wizard of Oz." When the movie surprisingly went from black and white to Technicolor, she leaned over to me and characteristically assured, "It's a dream" Over the next forty years during which time she and my dad raised five children, she was to clarify so many things: dreams, nightmares, heartaches, rapture!

It is easy, even after so many years, to recall the walk back home from some movie on a cold winter night with this young mother/woman then so strong, agile, and lithe. My small hand in hers, we both feigned lion courage as our boots crunched the cold snow and we walked through real or imaginary shadows.

As a youngster, I was always so eager to have her come to school activities. Taller than average, she would often wear wide-brimmed hats that lent her added grace. My heart would well up with pride and love as I saw her arrive through the crowd. "Hi, mom." She was already beautiful: there was actually never a reason for her to post handwritten signs on our refrigerator door intended to curb her love for food (and life): "Nobody loves a fatty."

How idyllic a world this centerpiece of our Shaker-clean home composed for us: delectable *pâtés* and *soufflés* (no recipe to speak of), player-piano-ed dusks, Sunday afternoon drives through Maine pines, Strauss, unconditional faith, Emily Post (*de rigeur*), starched or pressed home-made clothing, work ethic, Rodgers and Hammerstein wake-up calls to the smell of warm cinnamon coffee cake, and the high expectation always that we would return honor to the family.

With a little paint, a few yards of cloth, and her keen sense of comeliness, she could transform a gingham tenement into a taffeta manor.

How appreciative she was at the gift of even a single dandelion! How cheerful and non-complaining in all things! How caring of others with less, imploring: "What can I give you?…Take it; I don't really need it." How courageous in the teeth of challenge! How incredibly loving: "The longest part of my day is the ten minutes before your father arrives home from work."

After all these years, she seems like a lovely monarch butterfly God held in the palm of his hand.

Almost every afternoon of my high school days my mom, a cup of tea, and sweet colloquy awaited me. Later in life, the joy of that connection continued when I arrived home from work and heard her voice over my answering machine. Yes, it's a dream.

God never created a heart more tender than my mother's. Forever she will live in mine.

This is my everyday valentine to you, mom, with love.

(1968)

10

Happy Days

Now stir the fire, and close the shutters fast,
Let fall the curtains, wheel the sofa round,
And, while the bubbling and loud-hissing urn
Throws up a steamy column, and the cups,
That cheer but not inebriate, wait on each,
So let us welcome peaceful ev'ning in.

— WILLIAM COWPER

~ Happy Days ~

Sure, there's good television programming available around the holidays every year, but none quite so delightful as "The Perry Como Show" *aka* "The Chesterfield Supper Hour," *aka* "The Kraft Music Hall" during those halcyon days of the '50s.

I can sweetly remember the degree of anticipation with which we all approached these televised events – especially at Christmas and Thanksgiving. Lacking multiple television sets or addictive computers our entire family would gather in our Sanford, Maine den to enjoy the *avant-garde*, high tech medium of our 17-inch Philco television set.

Corn was popped for the occasion, and there was mercifully no regard for fat content, calories or points as melted butter richly streamed over the deliciously warm popcorn. Oh, and Kool-Aid all around.

Context, you ask? It was the best of times; it was the best of times. A Romantic mom who claimed the longest part of her day was the five minutes before my dad came home from work. A loving if matter-of-fact dad who was slowly transformed into a fan as the televised hour evolved.

Back to Perry, it wasn't only "good" television; it was inspiring television, "Mr. C.," as he was called at that venue, would open the show with his "Dream Along With Me" theme song.

It was true zeitgeist – the music of that time. It validated all of the hormone-popping sentiments of this teenager. Mitch Ayers served as musical director, and announcer Frank Gallop's sonorous bass voice, an invisible "voice from the clouds," was apt foil for Como's jokes.

Guests might include the likes of Kirk Douglas, whose beard former barber Perry Como shaved before our very eyes; Esther Williams or even Monaco's Prince Rainier and his bride, Grace Kelly.

Just about a half-hour into the show, you could find Perry dressed in a cardigan sweater now sitting on a stool, music stand before him, responding to song requests, having intoned "Sing To Me, Mr. C." And you could understand every word he sang – from "A Bushel and a Peck" to "Zing Zing-Zoom Zoom."

Before we knew it, the hour had almost passed, and it was time for Perry's culminating musical apotheosis, usually "Ave Maria" at Christmas (with Perry standing, say, in a ray of light before a stained-glass window) or "Bless This House" at Thanksgiving as he delivered this rousing prayer-song standing at the head of a colorful Thanksgiving table replete with harvest.

Alas, shortly after the program's end, we kiddos headed for a good night's sleep – complete with our Kool-Aid grape mustache. Yes, "Good night, Lorraine. Good night, Roland. Good night, mom."

That's really how it usually was. And it was pretty much the norm insofar as most of our neighbors and friends were concerned. Just ask the Pascucci's, McComb's, Roy's, Hough's and others who lived in that middle-class neighborhood.

Especially if U R a teen, I'll bet you've signed off reading this, say, four paragraphs ago. But OMG, I wish you that sense of belonging that we enjoyed, now acknowledging that all of these memories are envisioned through my fuddy-duddy (some would say "rose-colored") glasses. Believe me though, it was wicked cool! In fact, some of these neighbors truly continue to be BFFs.

It's with humility and thanksgiving that I recollect these happy memories, incredibly saddened because of much of today's dark pop (and sometimes absent Mom and Pop) culture. It was not a perfect life (Sister Mary Adolph: "It'll build your character"), but every member of the family knew their role, their lane and where the boundaries were. Actually, Perry's music affirmed all that.

"The Perry Como Show" was a kaleidoscope of the serious, comical, fun, inspiring, a family-binding WD-40 burst of entertainment. You might say a sacrament.

It's no wonder we call these "Happy Days."

(2013)

II

~ Interview ~

ON NOVEMBER 10, 1993,
THE EVE OF THEIR 60TH WEDDING
ANNIVERSARY,
MY PARENTS AGREED TO THE FOLLOWING
INTRIGUING INTERVIEW.
I NOTE THAT, NOTWITHSTANDING THEIR
LACK OF FORMAL EDUCATION AND WITH
ENGLISH AS A SECOND LANGUAGE,
NO QUESTION SPAWNED HESITATION;
NO FILTER; EVERY ANSWER A CLEAR MEMORY
OF THEIR RELATIONSHIP TO EACH OTHER,
TO FAMILY,
AND TO THIS GREAT COUNTRY!

~ 60ᵀʰ Anniversary Interview ~

QUESTION: WHAT'S YOUR NAME?
MOM: MY NAME IS LAURETTA BLANCHE CÔTÉ
DUTILE
DAD: INAUDIBLE

QUESTION: WHERE WERE YOU BORN?
MOM: I WAS BORN CINQUIÈME RANG [ROW]
ST. FABIEN, RIMOUSKI, PROVINCE DE QUÉBEC,
CANADA
DAD: BELMONT, NEW HAMPSHIRE

QUESTION: MOM, HOW DID YOUR FAMILY COME
TO THIS COUNTRY?
MY MOTHER KEPT SAYING SHE PASSED THE LINES
BY "EELAND POND." ONLY MY SISTER NITA SPOKE
ENGLISH THEN. BUT WILFRED [MY DAD] LOOKED
INTO IT WHEN I FILLED OUT MY CITIZEN PAPERS.
WE HAD THE HARDEST TIME. AND IT WAS REALLY
ISLAND POND [VERMONT].

QUESTION: DAD, WERE BOTH OF YOUR PARENTS BORN IN THIS COUNTRY?

NO. MY FATHER WAS BORN IN CRANBOURNE, AND MY MOTHER WAS BORN IN SACRÉ COEUR DE MARIE. THEY MET IN LACONIA AND MARRIED IN 1900.

QUESTION: HOW DID YOUR PARENTS GET HERE, MOM?

MOM: MUST HAVE COME BY TRAIN. THAT'S ALL THAT WAS RUNNING.

QUESTION: HOW MANY CHILDREN DID THEY HAVE AT THE TIME?

MOM: 9 CHILDREN AND 1 COMING – 1 IN THE OVEN

QUESTION: WHAT WAS YOUR FATHER'S PROFESSION?

MOM: MY FATHER WAS A FARMER AND WOODCUTTER.

QUESTION: LATER HE WORKED IN THE MILLS?

MOM: YES; IN THE BLEACHERY MILLS IN LEWISTON.

QUESTION: AND YOUR MOM?

MOM: MY MOTHER WORKED IN THE ANDROSCOGGIN & BATES MILLS.

QUESTION: DID YOUR PARENTS EVER GO TO SCHOOL?

MOM: MY PARENTS NEVER WENT TO SCHOOL IN THEIR LIFE. WHEN MY FATHER WORKED IN THE MILLS, THEY GAVE HIM A STENCIL AND PAINTBRUSH SO HE COULD MARK HIS WORK. "X" MEANT "JOE CÔTÉ." MY MOTHER AND DAD'S MOTHER READ THE FRENCH NEWSPAPER TO THEIR HUSBAND EVERY NIGHT.

DAD: I DON'T THINK MY PARENTS EVER WENT TO SCHOOL.

QUESTION: WHY DID BOTH WOMEN KNOW HOW TO READ AND WRITE, AND THEIR HUSBANDS DIDN'T?

MOM: [JOKINGLY] — 'CAUSE WOMEN ARE SMARTER THAN MEN.

DAD: [CHUCKLING] —THAT'S A LIE!

QUESTION: DAD, TAKE ME TO A TYPICAL DAY WHEN YOU WERE IN THE FIFTH GRADE.

DAD: UP AT 5:00 AM, MILK THE COWS, PULL THE COWS' TITS, WASH HANDS, BREAKFAST…

MOM: SEE? THAT'S SOMETHING I DIDN'T KNOW ABOUT.

QUESTION: TYPICAL BREAKFAST?

DAD: BAKED BEANS, EGGS, SALT PORK

QUESTION: HEARTY BREAKFAST?
DAD: OH, YES. HEARTY BREAKFAST.

QUESTION: AFTER BREAKFAST?
DAD: FEED THE CHICKENS, FEED THE PIGS, FILL BOTH STOVES (SMALL AND BIG) WITH WOOD.
MOM: DO YOU SEE THAT LITTLE FACE [TURNING TO HIM] DOING A DAY'S WORK BEFORE SCHOOL? AND HE HAD ASTHMA THEN.

QUESTION: YOU FORGOT SOMETHING?
DAD: WHAT?

QUESTION: CATECHISM?
DAD: THAT WAS AFTER SCHOOL.

QUESTION: YOU WALKED TO SCHOOL?
DAD: YES; IT WAS A MILE WALK EACH WAY. IT WAS 4.5 MILES TO HIGH SCHOOL.

QUESTION: WHAT WERE THE SCHOOL'S HOURS?
DAD: 8:30 TO 3:30

QUESTION: BY THE WAY, WHAT DID YOU DO FOR LUNCH?
DAD: MY MOTHER MADE SANDWICHES FOR 4 CHILDREN IN SCHOOL AND 3 ADULTS WHO LIVED AT HOME WITH HOME-MADE KETCHUP,

PORK BUTTS. I'M NOT KIDDING YOU, THE PORK BUTTS WERE HALF FAT. DELICIOUS!

QUESTION: AFTER SCHOOL?
DAD: CHANGE CLOTHES, PUT ON OUR FARMERS' CLOTHES. WE'D GO OUT AGAIN TO FEED THE CHICKENS, FEED THE PIGS, GET SOME WOOD. MY MOTHER WOULD TEACH US CATECHISM FOR 15 TO 20 MINUTES, KNIT, AND COOK SUPPER AT THE SAME TIME.

QUESTION: HEARTY SUPPER?
DAD: YES

QUESTION: AFTER SUPPER?
DAD: WE'D GO OUT AGAIN. CLEAN THE CACA OF THE COWS [STALLS], HAND-PUMP WATER FOR 20 COWS. THEY'D SEND 3 COWS AT A TIME. THEN WE'D HAVE TO PUMP MORE WATER.

QUESTION: HOMEWORK?
DAD: NO HOMEWORK.

QUESTION: WHAT TIME DID YOU GO TO BED?
DAD: 8:00

QUESTION: MOM, HOW ABOUT YOUR TYPICAL DAY IN THE FIFTH GRADE?

MOM: I DIDN'T HAVE A HARD TIME LIKE HE DID. GET UP, DRESS UP. WE'D TAKE THE 8:30 TROLLEY TO SCHOOL.

QUESTION: WHAT TIME DID IT START?
MOM: STARTED AT QUARTER OF NINE.

QUESTION: HEARTY BREAKFAST?
MOM: YOU BET! FRIED SALT PORK SLICES, TOAST, BAKED BEANS, EGGS. WE'D FILL UP THE BLACK TOP OF THE WOOD STOVE WITH BREAD AND MAKE TOAST. WHEN I WENT ON MY HONEYMOON, I SAID TO DAD, "I WANT A REAL TOAST." [MEANING COOKED IN A TOASTER]

QUESTION: WHAT DID YOU DO WHEN YOU CAME HOME FROM SCHOOL?
MOM: MOP THE ROOMS, SET THE TABLE, PEEL POTATOES FOR 13 PEOPLE. (MY MOTHER TOOK IN A BOARDER.} AFTER SUPPER, DO THE DISHES. A L'ÉCOLE PAROISSIALE [AT PAROCHIAL SCHOOL] WE HAD LOTS OF HOMEWORK. THEN WE WENT TO BED.

QUESTION: DESCRIBE A HAPPY MEMORY FROM YOUR CHILDHOOD.
MOM: MY MOTHER WAS SICK IN BED. HOW DO YOU CALL IT? PMS? VERY SICK. HER SKIN

WAS FULL OF RASH. EVA [HER DAUGHTER] WAS TAKING CARE OF HER. EVA MADE HER A STEAK WITH FRENCH FRIES. MY MOTHER BLOCKED. SHE COULDN'T GO TO THE BATHROOM. I WENT TO THE PORTLAND CATHEDRAL AND ASKED THE BLESSED MOTHER THAT MY MOTHER GET WELL. LATER, FATHER NADEAU CAME TO SEE HER. HE ASKED, "ÇA VA BIEN, MADAME CÔTÉ?" [YOU'RE DOING WELL, MRS. CÔTÉ ?] AND SHE RESPONDED, "NON, MON PÈRE; JE PEUX PAS ALLER À SEL." [NO, FATHER. I CANNOT SEEM TO HAVE A BOWEL MOVEMENT.] "AVEZ VOUS PRIS D'HUILE DE CASTOR?" [DID YOU TAKE SOME CASTOR OIL?] "OUI, MON PÈRE; J'AI TOUT ESSAYÉ." {YES, FATHER; I'VE TRIED EVERYTHING.] SHE LATER TOOK SOME CASTOR OIL AND WENT TO THE BATHROOM IMMEDIATELY. THAT PLEASED ME. DAD: THEY WERE ALL HAPPY.

QUESTION: DAD, TELL ME ABOUT A HAPPY DAY FROM YOUR CHILDHOOD?
DAD: OH, I HAD LOTS OF HAPPY DAYS.
MOM: WHAT ABOUT SATURDAY NIGHT?
DAD: WHEN I WAS OLDER ON SATURDAY NIGHT WE HAD THE MODEL T FORD."

QUESTION: HOW OLD?
DAD: 14 TO 16

QUESTION: DID YOU PICK UP GIRLS?
DAD: NO.

QUESTION: TELL ME ONE THING YOU'D CHANGE ABOUT YOUR CHILDHOOD?
MOM: I USED TO THINK IF I WAS A CHILD AGAIN: WHY DID I GO WITH ANY BOYS AT ALL? WHY DIDN'T I WAIT FOR WILFRED? WE WERE ALWAYS GETTING READY TO GET MARRIED. "YOU'RE TOO YOUNG." SO WE'D START OVER AGAIN. MY FATHER DIED MARCH 22; WE [THEN-FIANCÉ REYNOLD AND SHE] WERE SUPPOSED TO GET MARRIED MAY 30TH, BUT YOU DON'T GET MARRIED WHEN YOU'RE IN MOURNING. REYNOLD LATER WENT TO CHICAGO TO LEARN TO FIX RADIOS. THEN THIS ONE [DAD] CAME ALONG. ALSO, I USED TO SAY, WHY AREN'T I LIKE NITA [HER SISTER]? WE WERE INSEPARABLE, NITA AND ME. WE'D GO TO THE DANCE, AND SHE WAS SUPPOSED TO BE HOME EARLIER BECAUSE SHE WAS YOUNGER SO I WOULD BEG HER TO TAKE THE LAST TROLLEY AT 11:00 PM. SHE'D SAY, "I'M STAYING." MY FRIENDS WOULD HAVE TAKEN ME HOME LATER. SO I'D HAVE TO LEAVE THE DANCE EARLY ON THE 11:00 TROLLEY SO SHE'D BE HOME ON TIME. WHENEVER I WANTED TO

GO SOMEWHERE, I'D ASK MY MOM, "CAN I GO?" THE ANSWER WAS OFTEN, "RESTES IÇI; T'AS PAS D'AFFAIRE LA!" [STAY HOME; YOU DON'T HAVE ANY BUSINESS THERE.} SO I'D STAY HOME. NITA WOULD JUST SAY, "MA, I'M GOING HERE OR THERE." BUT TODAY I'M GLAD I TREATED MY MOTHER THAT WAY.

QUESTION: DAD, ONE THING YOU'D CHANGE ABOUT YOUR CHILDHOOD?
DAD: THE NEIGHBORS, THE GILBERT'S, USED TO WORK IN THE MILLS AND HAVE A PAYCHECK. WE HAD TO WORK ON THE FARM WITH NO PAYCHECK.

QUESTION: WHAT ARE TWO WORDS TO DESCRIBE YOU?
DAD: I DON'T THINK ONE PERSON CAN DESCRIBE HIMSELF.
MOM: TWO WORDS. I'M VERY NICE. [LAUGHING] I THINK I'M BETTER THAN PEOPLE THINK. PRIDE I HAVE. I HAVE A HEART. THERE WERE TWO WOMEN ON TV FIGHTING FOR A MAN WHO GOT THREE WOMEN PREGNANT.
DAD: LUCKY GUY!
MOM: DO YOU THINK I'D STAND FOR THAT. "BUT I LOVE HIM." CRAZY WOMAN!

QUESTION: TELL ME ABOUT THE CATHOLIC CHURCH?

MOM: I THINK THE CATHOLIC CHURCH, NOT JUST THE CATHOLIC CHURCH, MAKES PEOPLE BETTER. WITHOUT ANY KIND OF RELIGION, PEOPLE WOULD BE WORSE THAN THEY ARE.

QUESTION: YOUR PARENTS WERE VERY RELIGIOUS?

MOM: AH, JESUS DE PLATE! CHAPELETS [ROSARY BEADS SAID AS A FAMILY ON YOUR KNEES] EVERY NIGHT AFTER SUPPER.] DES GROSSES FAMILLES. [BIG FAMILIES.]

DAD: VERY RELIGIOUS

QUESTION: YOU WENT TO MASS EVERY SUNDAY?

DAD: NOT WHEN IT WAS TOO SNOWY. WE COULDN'T GET TO THE CHURCH.

MOM: WE SAID LONG PRAYERS [DECADES OF THE ROSARY INCLUDING THE CREED]. WE'D GO TO THE CHILDREN'S MASS AND AFTER MASS WE'D SAY MORE LONG PRAYERS. WHEN IT CAME TO CONRAD [YOUNGER BROTHER] WHO WAS 8 YEARS OLD, HE WOULD AGAIN START THE CHAPELET [ROSARY] WITH THE LONG PRAYERS. HE NEVER MISSED A WORD. WE THOUGHT HE WAS KIND OF CUTE.

DAD: YES, THE ROSARY WAS STARTED BY MY FATHER, THEN MY MOTHER, THEN EACH KID. AFTER THE ROSARY, MORE LONG PRAYERS: "O MON DIEU, JE VOUS DONNE MON COEUR, MON ÂME... [OH, MY GOD, I GIVE YOU MY HEART, MY SOUL...]

QUESTION: DID YOU FEEL CLOSE TO THE CHURCH GROWING UP?
MOM: IT WAS A MUST.
DAD: YES, BECAUSE EVERYBODY DID. I REMEMBER WHEN WE WERE YOUNG, WE WENT TO MASS AND DIDN'T HAVE ANY MONEY FOR THE COLLECTION, FATHER WOULD KNOCK YOUR KNUCKLES WITH THE COLLECTION BASKET.
MOM: YES, IN FACT YOU SAID YOU JOINED THE CHOIR SO THAT YOU WOULD NOT BE EMBARRASSED.

QUESTION: DID ANY OF YOUR SIBLINGS HAVE A HIGH SCHOOL DIPLOMA?
MOM: WHEN MY SISTER NITA GRADUATED FROM THE EIGHTH GRADE, SHE WANTED TO GO TO HIGH SCHOOL. SHE WAS THE SMARTEST ONE. MY MOTHER TOLD HER, "YOU CAN GO TO HIGH SCHOOL, NITA, BUT DON'T THINK YOUR SISTERS ARE GOING TO WORK IN THE MILLS TO DRESS YOU UP." SO SHE DIDN'T GO. WE HAD TO WORK.

DAD: WHEN MY BROTHER, DELPHIS, WAS SUPPOSED TO GO TO HIGH SCHOOL, HE DIDN'T. HE HAD TO WORK ON THE FARM. VERY FEW OF US HAD AN 8TH GRADE DIPLOMA.

QUESTION: WHY DID YOU VALUE EDUCATION SO MUCH?

MOM: 'CAUSE WILFRED DID. I WAS RAISED TO THINK THAT A GUY WHO WENT TO COLLEGE WAS LAZY, A GUY WHO WENT IN THE SERVICE WAS A BUM, AND A BUSINESSMAN WAS A CROOK. I HAD A DATE ONCE WITH A COLLEGE GUY. MY DAD SAID HE WAS A LAZY GUY. SO I STAYED HOME. THAT'S THE WAY WE WERE BROUGHT UP, BUT HE [WILFRED] CHANGED MY MIND SOON AFTER WE WERE MARRIED. HIS UNCLES SUFFERED A LOT BECAUSE OF NO EDUCATION SO THEY WENT TO SCHOOL AT NIGHT.

DAD: BECAUSE I LACKED IT.

QUESTION: ARE YOU PROUD OF YOUR FRENCH LINEAGE?

MOM: I'M VERY PROUD, BUT I WAS PROUD THAT I WAS A CANADIAN CITIZEN. WHEN I BECAME A NATURALIZED CITIZEN, THE JUDGE SAID THAT OUR ORIGINAL COUNTRY [CANADA] WAS LIKE OUR PARENTS, AND THAT OUR NEW COUNTRY [UNITED STATES] WAS LIKE SOMEONE

YOU MARRY. WHEN YOU MARRY, YOU DON'T HATE YOUR PARENTS SO YOU SHOULD ALSO CONTINUE LOVING YOUR FORMER COUNTRY. ALWAYS THINK OF YOUR COUNTRY AS A GOOD COUNTRY.
DAD: VERY PROUD

QUESTION: HOW DID YOU MEET?
DAD: I WAS BOARDING AT HER SISTER'S [MARY} HOUSE.
MOM: I WENT TO MARY'S TO GET A HAIRCUT AND SAW HIS PICTURE ON THE BUREAU.

QUESTION: AS A FRANCO-AMERICAN, DID YOU EXPERIENCE PREJUDICE?
MOM: WE SURE DID. WHEN WE MOVED TO PLEASANT STREET [LEWISTON, MAINE] ONE NIGHT ABOUT 10:00 PM, SOME GUYS THREW SOME BIG ROCKS ON OUR PORCH ON ACCOUNT OF WE WERE CATHOLICS. THEY HATED CATHOLICS. DAD LIVED ON A FARM; THEY DIDN'T SEE THAT.

QUESTION: AND, DAD, I REMEMBER YOUR TELLING ABOUT WHEN YOU BOUGHT THE GROCERY STORE IN GOFFSTOWN, NH?
DAD: VERY MUCH PREJUDICE. THEY STOPPED ME WHEN I WAS REMODELING OUTSIDE OF MY GROCERY STORE AND ASKED ME WHY I WAS

MOVING THERE. THEY SAID THEY DIDN'T NEED ANY CATHOLICS IN TOWN.

QUESTION: YOU WERE MARRIED 60 YEARS AGO TOMORROW, NOVEMBER 11, 1933.
DAD: YES, NOVEMBER 11, 1933. WE MADE PEACE.

QUESTION: WHY DID YOU DECIDE TO MOVE TO SANFORD [MAINE – 1947]
MOM: HE WANTED A BUSINESS..
DAD: IT WAS A SMALL TOWN AND A CHANGE.

QUESTION: YOU BELIEVED IN PAROCHIAL SCHOOLS?
MOM: YOU BET YOUR LIFE! WE STILL DO!
DAD: YOU BET YOUR LIFE!

QUESTION: WAS THERE A CHANCE OF PROMOTION AT YOUR WORK?
MOM: YES, POSSIBLE. ONCE IN A WHILE, WE'D GET TWO CENTS MORE.

QUESTION: I MEAN A PROMOTION, NOT A RAISE.
MOM: FOR COLLEGE PEOPLE, YES. BUT NOT FOR PEOPLE LIKE ME. NONE OF THE BOSSES WERE FRENCH.
DAD: IF YOU WERE NOT FRENCH, IT WAS EASIER TO BE PROMOTED. BUT I REMEMBER JOE

SIMARD. HE WAS FRENCH —- MY SUPERVISOR AND A SLAVE DRIVER. HE DROVE ME DAY AFTER DAY.

QUESTION: WHO DID WHAT WHERE YOU WORKED?
MOM: MEN SWEPT, LOADED BOXES, WOMEN STITCHED. THE MEN MADE THE BOTTOM OF THE SHOE AND THE WOMEN DID THE TOP. IF I HAD MY WAY, I'D STILL BE THERE WORKING.
DAD: REMEMBER THAT THERE WERE VERY FEW WOMEN WORKING THEN — MAYBE 15%. THEY ALSO FOLDED CLOTH.

QUESTION: WHAT MAKES A GOOD MARRIAGE?
MOM: I THINK A GOOD MARRIAGE IS LIKE OUR MARRIAGE (HA, HA), THE MAN TAKES, AND I GIVE.
DAD: MANY REASONS. FIDELITY IS ONE. BEING A DECENT WAGE-EARNER. I WORKED FOR 25 CENTS AN HOUR PAINTING, WALLPAPERING. I WALLPAPERED A WHOLE ROOM FOR $2. DOING GOOD THINGS FOR EACH OTHER IS ANOTHER. COMPASSION.

QUESTION: WERE YOU CLOSER TO YOUR MOM OR DAD? IF YOU WERE PREGNANT OR CAUSED SOMEONE TO BE PREGNANT BEFORE MARRIAGE,

WHOM WOULD YOU HAVE TOLD FIRST? YOUR MOTHER OR FATHER?
DAD: I WAS CLOSER TO MY MOTHER.

QUESTION: YOU'D TELL YOUR MOTHER FIRST?
DAD: YES, I THINK SO.

QUESTION: MOM, YOU'RE PREGNANT. WHOM DO YOU TELL?
MOM: (JOKING) NO ONE. NOT EVEN THE DOCTOR. LAURIANNE, MY GIRLFRIEND, TOLD ME ABOUT HER SISTER WHO HAD A BABY. I WAS 8 OR 9. SHE SAID HER SISTER HAD A BABY BECAUSE SHE RAN TOO MUCH. I HAD RUN ALL MORNING AT RECESS. I WENT CRAZY THINKING I WAS GOING TO HAVE A BABY. MY MOTHER USED TO SAY SHE'D HAVE A LITTLE PACKAGE AT THE DOOR FOR US IF WE GOT PREGNANT.
DAD: I NEVER HEARD MY MOTHER SAY THAT.
MOM: I WANTED TO THROW MYSELF IN THE CANAL. THEN MY GIRLFRIEND TOLD ME WHAT YOU REALLY HAD TO DO TO GET PREGNANT. OH, WHAT A RELIEF THAT WAS TO HEAR. I KNEW THE BABY WAS COMING BY THE BUTTONHOLE. THEN I STARTED TO HAVE LITTLE BUTTONS [BREASTS], AND THEY WERE KIDDING ME. TO TELL YOU THE TRUTH, I NEVER REALLY HAD BREASTS (HA, HA)

QUESTION: HOW MANY BROTHERS AND SISTERS?
DAD: 8 OF US IN ALL.

QUESTION: NAME THEM?
DAD: HENRY [THEN DECEASED], DELPHIS, HOMER, RAYMOND, LEO [THEN DECEASED], YVONNE, AMEDÉE, NORA

QUESTION: MOM, HOW MANY BROTHERS AND SISTERS?
MOM: 4 BROTHERS AND 5 SISTERS.

QUESTION: NAME THEM?
WELL, OF COURSE, ALL OF THEM CHANGED THEIR NAME TO GO TO WORK. WE USED OUR CANADIAN RELATIVES' BIRTH CERTIFICATES IN THE STATES TO LIE THAT WE WERE 16 YEARS OLD AND COULD LEGALLY WORK. YVONNE, EVA, MARIA, CONRAD, ARMAND, DESIRÉ, JOSEPH, ANITA, MEDORA.

QUESTION: TELL ME SOMETHING IN YOUR LIFE YOU'RE PROUD OF?
MOM: WHEN I MET WILFRED, I WAS ENGAGED TO BE MARRIED. I HAD TO MAKE 3 WISHES [?]. "I SAID I WISH I WOULD MARRY WILFRED DUTILE." DAD: IT WOULD BE NICE IF I SAID I MARRIED HER, WOULDN'T IT?

QUESTION: THE HAPPIEST MEMORY IN YOUR ADULT LIFE?
DAD: MANY. I HAD A LOT OF HAPPY MEMORIES. WHEN I SOLD MY SHOE STORE. I WAS TIRED. WHEN I SOLD MY COTTAGE…"

QUESTION: WHY NOT WHEN YOU GOT YOUR COTTAGE?
DAD: OH, THAT'S TRUE. WE HAD A LOT OF GOOD TIMES THERE. WHEN I OPENED MY BIG SHOE STORE IN SANFORD. THAT WAS A NICE STORE. I WAS FOOLISH THAT WAY. I HAD MY LITTLE STORE [ON WASHINGTON STREET IN SANFORD] FOR THREE YEARS. I WAS IN BED ONE NIGHT, IN MY MIND I WENT THROUGH ALL THE BUSINESSES ON MAIN STREET TO GUESS WHICH BUSINESS I COULD REPLACE SO I'D HAVE A BETTER LOCATION. AFTER A WHILE, I SAID TO MYSELF, WHAT IS WATKINS CLEANERS DOING ON MAIN STREET WITH THAT HIGH RENT? THEY BELONG IN MY STORE WITH $75/MONTH RENT. I CALLED THE HEAD OF THE COMPANY IN PORTLAND. THEY REALLY WANTED OUT, BUT THEY DIDN'T WANT MY SMALL STORE. THEY TOLD ME IF THEY COULD BE RELEASED FROM THEIR LEASE WITH GEORGE CLARK [BUILDING PROPRIETOR], I COULD HAVE THE STORE. GEORGE CLARK AGREED. HE ADDED, "WATKINS WAS SUPPOSED

TO DO A LOT OF THINGS TO IMPROVE THAT STORE, BUT THEY DIDN'T." THE BUILDING WAS OLD, RATS RUNNNG AROUND EVERYWHERE. NO CELLAR. I SAID TO GEORGE CLARK, "IF YOU BUILD ME A NEW STORE, I'LL PAY YOU $4,000." [$39,835 IN 2016] HE DIDN'T SEEM IMPRESSED. HE WENT TO HIS LAWYER, GEORGE WILLARD, WHO TOLD HIM, "DON'T BE A FOOL. HE'S WILLING TO PAY 1/3 OF THE WHOLE COST OF THE NEW BUILDING." GEORGE CLARK AGREED AGAIN. THE LAMONTAGNES BUILT IT AT A TOTAL COST OF $12,000 [$119,506], BUT I BOUGHT A LOT OF THINGS LIKE THE LIGHT FIXTURES MYSELF. GEORGE CLARK RAISED MY RENT FROM $150 TO $225. THAT WASN'T IN THE TERMS. I USED TO TALK TO JOHN PAPAS [SUCCESSFUL SANFORD BUSINESS PROPRIETOR] AND TOOK HIS ADVICE ABOUT BUSINESS. I TRIED TO DO WHAT THE BIG STORES DID. JOHN PAPAS HAD A LEASE WITH THE FIRST NATIONAL, AND THEY, AS LESSORS, HAD PAID FOR THE ENTIRE COST OF MR. PAPAS' BUILDING.

QUESTION: HOW LONG WAS THAT LEASE?
DAD: 5 AND 5. I DIDN'T WANT TO GO TOO FAR..

QUESTION: YOU DID PRETTY WELL THOUGH…
DAD: OH, YES. NO COMPLAINTS.

QUESTION: MOM, A HAPPY ADULT MEMORY?
MOM: OH, THAT'S SO EASY TO SAY. I HAD MANY OF THEM. WHEN I HAD MY FIRST CHILD, IT WAS A GIRL. DAD WOULD BRING HER TO ME AND SAY, "BABY YOU GOT YOUR LITTLE GIRL." "VAS DONC CHERCHER LA PETITE," [WHY DON'T YOU GET THE LITTLE ONE?] I KEPT ASKING. SHE LOOKED JUST LIKE MY SISTER, YVONNE. SHE WAS BORN DURING A THUNDERSTORM SO THERE WERE CANDLES IN THE ROOM. DAD THOUGHT THAT, IF I WOKE UP FROM THE CHLOROFORM, I'D THINK I WAS DYING. HE NEVER LEFT ME. THE SECOND CHILD WAS A BOY, A BIG DISAPPOINTMENT. BUT ONE DAY NORA [SISTER-IN-LAW] CAME OVER, AND SHE THOUGHT HE WAS ADORABLE. WHEN I WAS CHANGING HIS DIAPER, HE PEED IN MY FACE. I TURNED TO DAD AND ASKED, "WHO DID THAT?" WE LAUGHED SO MUCH. THEN I KNEW HE WOULD BE "MES POTEAUX DE VIELLESSE" [PILLARS OF OLD AGE]. I WAS CRAZY ABOUT HIM!

QUESTION: DESCRIBE RICHARD [OLDEST SON]?
MOM: HE WAS TANANT [NAUGHTY]. NOT NOW; IL EST TROP VIEUX. IL PEUX PU GROUYER. [HE'S TOO OLD AND CAN'T MOVE.] SO GOOD-HEARTED, ALWAYS WONDERFUL. RICHARD WAS ALWAYS FAST AND DID THE WORK. HE'D QUESTION BUZZY [FERNAND/TEX, THE

SECOND OLDEST BROTHER] "BUZZY, WHY DON'T YOU HELP MAMA?" HE'D DO THE DISHES WHEN I WAS GETTING THE KIDS READY FOR SCHOOL AND DAD WENT TO MANCHESTER TO GET SOME MEAT FOR THE GROCERY STORE. TEX USED TO SAY, "ASK ME IF YOU WANT SOMETHING DONE, MOM. I DON'T THINK LIKE RICHARD DOES."

DAD: I FEEL LIKE YOUR MOTHER DOES. RICHARD HAS A HEART OF GOLD, VERY AMBITIOUS AND SO GENEROUS.

QUESTION: DESCRIBE TEX [SECOND OLDEST SON]?
MOM: WELL, TEX...

QUESTION: MOM, LET HIM [DAD] GO FIRST. HE'S BEEN HANGING BACK LETTING YOU ANSWER FIRST THEN JUST AGREEING WITH YOU.

DAD: TEX IS A DIFFERENT GUY. WELL, NO ONE CAN EXPLAIN IT AS GOOD AS THEIR MOTHER CAN.

MOM: DON'T SAY THAT! YOU PAID ALL THE BILLS. YOU PAID FOR EVERYTHING.

DAD: TEX WAS OPEN-MINDED. HE REALLY WANTED TO GO TO SCHOOL. HE GRADUATED AS A LAWYER, AND HE REALLY WANTED TO GO TO SCHOOL. MORE THAN ANY OTHERS DID AT THE

TIME. NOT AS AMBITIOUS AS THE OTHERS ARE. HE IS IN THE CORRECT POSITION.

MOM: OH, DON'T SAY THAT. HE DOES ALL THAT RESEARCH IN THOSE BOOKS. HE WORKS HARD. I LOOKED IN THE DICTIONARY FOR EVERY WORD HE WROTE. HE'S IN HIS PROFESSION. HE WOULDN'T BE GOOD WITH A SHOVEL. YOU COULD HAVE GIVEN HIM ANYTHING TO WEAR OR EAT. I'D ASK, "ARE YOU GOING TO WEAR SHORT PANTS?" HE NEVER KICKED ABOUT FOOD OR CLOTHES. "IF THEY SEE ME, THEY'LL WEAR SHORT PANTS TOO," HE'D ANSWER.

QUESTION: DESCRIBE WILLIE [THIRD OLDEST SON]?

MOM: WILLIE IS VERY SENSIBLE [FRENCH FOR "SENSITIVE"]. HE IS ANOTHER THAT IS ALWAYS IN FRONT OF ME. I WENT TO HIS HOUSE, HE TREATED ME LIKE A QUEEN. HE WAS ALWAYS IN FRONT OF ME. HE SET UP A TV IN A BEDROOM ON THE FIRST FLOOR AT HIS HOUSE. DAVID [FOURTH SON] WILL PASS BY THE GARBAGE CAN 100 TIMES, BUT WILLIE SEES WHAT HAS TO BE DONE. WILLIE'S ANOTHER ONE WHO SEES WHAT HAS TO BE DONE.

QUESTION: DESCRIBE DAVID [YOUNGEST CHILD]?

MOM: DAVID IS A LITTLE DOLL. SOMETIMES HE CAN PUT YOU IN THE GRAVE. BECAUSE OF ALL

THE THINGS HE DOES. IF EVERYBODY HAD A CHILD LIKE THAT, HE'S VERY, VERY NICE.

DAD: HE'S SO KNOWLEDGEABLE ABOUT EVERYTHING. IF YOU DON'T GET ALONG WITH DAVID, YOU DON'T GET ALONG WITH ANYONE.

QUESTION: DESCRIBE LORRAINE?

MOM: LORRAINE, ET MAUDIT, [OH, DAMN] LORRAINE, WHAT CAN I SAY? WE USED TO HAVE A LOT OF FUN TOGETHER! WHEN SHE WAS YOUNG I USED TO LISTEN TO A RADIO PROGRAM, "WINNER TAKE ALL," IN THE MORNING WHILE I DID THE HOUSEWORK. IN THE AFTERNOON WHEN SHE CAME HOME FROM SCHOOL, THE SAME PROGRAM REPEATED. I KNEW ALL THE ANSWERS. AND SHE COULDN'T GET OVER IT. SHE KEPT SAYING, "MAMA, ARE YOU SMART!" DO YOU REMEMBER WHAT WE USED TO EAT A LOT, LORRAINE? A LOT OF CHINESE CABBAGE, HAMBURGERS. SOMETIMES SHE WOULD BE A LITTLE FREECASSAGE – GET MAD EASILY, BUT SHE GOT OVER IT FAST. SHE WOULD DO THE HOUSEWORK UPSTAIRS AND MARK THE TOWELS "DO NOT USE THESE." SHE HATED TO WASH TOILETS, BUT SHE IS A HARD WORKER AND VERY NEAT.

DAD: WHAT A HARD WORKER, VERY AMBITIOUS!

MOM: WHEN IT WAS WINDY, I'D TAKE ALL OF THE BEDSPREADS OFF THE BEDS AND PUT THEM

ON THE LINE TO AIR OUT. WHEN I SEWED, I WOULD COMPLETE THE COAT IN ONE DAY. BUT I WOULD THROW ALL THE REMNANTS AND TRIMMINGS ALL OVER THE FLOOR. ONE DAY LORRAINE CAME HOME FROM SCHOOL, SAW THAT THE BEDS HAD NO SPREADS AND SAW THE MESS I HAD MADE. SHE STARTED CRYING, "LOOK AT THIS HOUSE! "

QUESTION: WHAT DO YOU WANT PEOPLE TO REMEMBER ABOUT YOU?

DAD: THE DAY OF THE BURIAL.

MOM: HE'S ALWAYS IN THE GUTTER. THAT'S WHY HE'S SICK.

DAD: WELL, THAT'S WHERE WE'RE ALL GOING.

MOM: WE'LL GET THERE WHEN WE GET THERE. I'M WALKING VERY SLOW.. I'D LIKE PEOPLE TO SAY, "SHE WASN'T BAD." I DON'T WANT THE KIDS TO HATE ME. "YOU KNOW, MY MOM WASN'T THAT BAD." PRIDE I HAVE, BUT I'M BETTER THAN PEOPLE THINK I AM. I HAVE A HEART.

DAD: I FEEL THE SAME WAY. I DID THE BEST I COULD.

MOM: I'M TELLING YOU THAT WHEN WE STARTED OUR MARRIAGE, LORRAINE NEEDED PICHOUS [SLIPPERS] THAT COST 20 CENTS. WE DIDN'T HAVE IT. WE HAD A HARD TIME. I WOULD TAKE

ALL OF THE LEFTOVERS IN THE REFRIGERATOR, RIGHT, DAD?, MIX THEM IN A DISH, PUT A CRUST OVER THEM, AND IT WAS DELICIOUS.

QUESTION: ANYTHING ELSE YOU'D LIKE ME TO ASK YOU?

MOM: WELL, WE HAD A BEAUTIFUL TIME TONIGHT. WE HAVE A BEAUTIFUL FAMILY. I'M THANKING ALL THE KIDS FOR SUCH A NICE TIME.

DAD: I WISH YOU WOULD ASK ME WHAT A FOOLISH THING I DID. (LIKE WHEN SHE MARRIED ME. HA, HA) IN CLAREMONT, NEW HAMPSHIRE WHERE WE LIVED, I HAD A BEAUTIFUL GOVERNMENT JOB [IRS], LEFT IT WITH 4 KIDS, BOUGHT A GROCERY STORE IN GOFFSTOWN, NEW HAMPSHIRE FILLED WITH LITTLE MORE THAN $300 WORTH OF CEREALS AND SOLD ALL THE INVENTORY FOR $45. THE OWNER HAD A GUY, MR. SARGENT, WHO DROVE A TRUCK $13/WEEK TO DELIVER LITTLE MORE THAN A BOTTLE OF KETCHUP EVERY DAY AND A WOMAN TO KEEP BOOKS (STORE GROSSED ONLY ABOUT $300 A WEEK). I GOT RID OF THEM. I STARTED WORKING EVERY NIGHT AND TURNED THE GENERAL STORE INTO A MODERN IGA STORE.

QUESTION: TELL ME ABOUT A BAD DECISION?

DAD: SELLING MY CAMP AT WELLS FOR $17,500. DAVID SAID THEY MADE 2 CONDOS OUT OF IT AND SOLD EACH FOR $175,000.

MOM: HE'S LIVING IN THE PAST, YOUR FATHER. I DON'T THINK I EVER DID A FOOLISH THING. [LAUGHING]

QUESTION: HOW DID YOU EVER LEARN TO SEW SUCH A THING AS A MACKINAW?

MOM: THAT WAS MY TRADE. I WAS AT THE SHOP PUTTING BLACK ON SHOES, AND I WANTED TO SEW. THE SUPER SAID, "I ADMIRE FRENCH GIRLS. ONE OF THEM CAME IN AND SAID SHE WAS A GOOD STITCHER. SHE NEVER SAW A NEEDLE IN HER LIFE. I KEPT HER BECAUSE SHE WANTED TO LEARN. AND THEN I ADMIRED HER." ONE DAY IT WAS ON THE PAPER THAT CUSHMAN-HOLLIS WANTED 16 GIRLS TO LEARN TO SEW. I APPLIED AND LEARNED THERE. AFTER THAT, I BOUGHT A PATTERN. I MADE ALL OF YOUR CLOTHES INCLUDING CAPS FOR THE BOYS. ONE TIME A GUY HAD HIS INCOME TAX DONE WHERE DAD WORKED. HE ASKED DAD, "IS THAT YOUR CAR OVER THERE? I BUMPED IT." HE WAS WORKING IN THE MILL AND GAVE US A BIG ROLL OF KHAKI CLOTH THAT WAS USED TO DRESS YOU KIDS FOR YEARS JUST BECAUSE OF THAT BUMP.

QUESTION: DAD, HOW DID YOU LEARN CARPENTRY?

MOM: EVERYBODY WAS DOING IT THEN.

DAD: I'M NOT REALLY A GOOD CARPENTER. JUST LEARNED BY DOING IT.

QUESTION: HOW DID YOU GET ALL OF YOUR SMARTS?

DAD: WHAT SMARTS? I WORKED AT THE NAVY YARD. HAD TO WORK 10 WEEKS FREE TO LEARN HOW TO RUN A MACHINE TO GET THE JOB OF MACHINE OPERATOR. AFTER THAT, I WAS PROMOTED TO 3RD CLASS MACHINIST. WE WORKED 3 MONTH SHIFTS, AND IT WAS TOO MUCH FOR ME. I WAS DYING. MY FACE WOULD FALL ON THE LATHE. WE WORKED 13 DAYS WITHOUT STOPPING. TWO DAYS OFF A MONTH. 1 DAY OFF EVERY 2 WEEKS. WE'D GET PAID IF WE WERE SICK, BUT WE HAD TO BRING A DOCTOR'S CERTIFICATE TO RETURN TO WORK. GAVE MY NOTICE DURING THE WAR. I WAS MAKING $60 PER WEEK.

MOM: HE WAS SO SICK ONCE, AND THEY CAME TO CHECK ON HIM.

DAD: MY BOSS SAID IF YOU GET THROUGH WE'LL DRAFT YOU. AND THEY DID DRAFT ME. I HAD GONE TO THE LAHEY CLINIC FOR BLOOD WORK FOR MY ASTHMA. WHEN THE [MILITARY]

DOCTOR SAW THE TEST RESULTS, HE SAID, "WE CAN'T HAVE SICK PEOPLE ON THE FRONT LINES." SO I WAS CLASSIFIED 4F WHICH MADE US VERY HAPPY.

MOM: THAT WAS THE FIRST TIME I MISSED MY EDUCATION. DURING THE WAR WE WERE SUPPOSED TO SAY HOW BIG YOUR ROOMS WERE, AND I COULDN'T FIGURE OUT HOW TO DO IT.

DAD: CUBIC FEET IS WHAT SHE'S TALKING ABOUT. SO ALL I COULD GET FOR A JOB AFTER THE NAVY YARD WAS AT MONTGOMERY WARD'S FOR $35. EVERYTHING THEN WAS CONTRACTS WITH THE GOVERNMENT. FINALLY, ONE NIGHT I HAD THE GALL TO CALL THE NEW HAMPSHIRE DIRECTOR OF THE INTERNAL REVENUE SERVICE, PETER GAGNÉ OF SOMERSWORTH, AND TOLD HIM WHAT I WANTED TO DO – WORK FOR THE IRS. HE CALLED ME IN AND SAID, "I'D LIKE TO HIRE MORE FRENCH PEOPLE, BUT THEY DON'T COME. GO TO THE POST OFFICE AND TAKE THE EXAM. IF YOU PASS, I'LL HIRE YOU." I NEVER THOUGHT I'D GET IN 'CAUSE THERE WERE COLLEGE GUYS TAKING THE EXAM. I CAME IN SECOND! FOR EXAMPLE, THEY ASKED, "WHEN WAS THE LAST TIME YOU PAID INCOME TAX?" I NEVER DID; I MADE $1 AN HOUR ON MY TRUCK. NOT TOO MANY FRENCH GUYS LIKE MYSELF WITH NO EDUCATION WOULD TRY TO DO THAT, YOU

KNOW. HONEST TO GOD I DID THAT! I STILL HAVE MY IRS CERTIFICATE (CHUCKLING) IN CASE I WANT TO GO TO WORK.

QUESTIONER: YOU HAVE GIVEN US SOME GREAT INFORMATION ABOUT YOUR LIFE, YOUR VALUES. THANKS VERY MUCH, MOM AND DAD.
MOM: YOU'RE VERY WELCOME, LORRAINE. IT WAS A PLEASURE!
DAD: YES, THANK YOU.

12

Sommaire*

*You may ask, how did this tradition start? I'll
tell you —
I don't know.
But it's a tradition...*

— Tevye: Fiddler on the Roof

---

* SUMMARY

~ Sommaire ~

ALTHOUGH "HISTORIAN" SEEMS far more romantic and academic a descriptor than does "storyteller," I repeat that I think of myself more the latter. In summary, I look back across the crescent of the many stories told here, beginning in 1912, when my grandparents — the original dreamers — left an agrarian lifestyle that was sorely dependent on weather and on several other factors out of their control (for example, their English/Canadian partisan government) in order to travel a short distance from St. Fabien, Rimouski, Province de Quebec, Canada to Lewiston, Maine in the United States of America! Worthy of repetition:

> They left an agrarian way of life that included farming and woodcutting to put down roots (or perhaps the literal opposite) in this country at a time when The Mechanical Age excitedly beckoned. And although their remote vision of the good life was likely, romantically glossed over in Technicolor hues, their reasoning of a guaranteed paycheck from the mills

and textile places that glowingly tantalized them — as opposed to the fickle outcomes of farming dependent on weather and crops — was soundly grounded in reality.

And it wasn't only standard of living that attracted them, but as well the rich culture (quality of life) that through their peasant lens seemed inherently American. The courage they embodied was amazing!

The very title, "Growing Up Franco-American," because of its employed verb tense, grammatically infers a continuing action. Hence, it seems logical to carry this narrative to the next decimal place of life (mixing metaphors here) yea, to today, only two generations later on average. For crying out loud, at this age, I am or have *grown*! And, were I to become American Chief Surveyor of today's Franco-Americans, would I prejudicially be grading "on a curve" in this very personal case? Conversely, *isn't it really the narrative that is carrying/driving me* — as much for my own enlightenment as for that of those persevering readers who have followed me this far?

My intention here is less to compose some artificial, static outcome of this *memoir* than it is to update my story.

Fast-forwarding to today, what of it all? What part did this Franco ethnicity, as considered in a general sense across so many such immigrants, with all of its sometimes unorthodox orthodoxy, play out in this country? Surely, the ramifications on all levels are varied, but what aspects are positive; are today's Franco-Americans living happily after? More importantly, what have they contributed? Happy endings are never assured where human beings are concerned. Anyhow, the Franco-American narrative, if admittedly muted, is hardly ended.

Of course, I always have the opportunity of gazing across the horizon at my own biological siblings (four brothers), my compatriots or *confrères,* and their progeny since I interact with many of them in my everyday life. At this age, many of my generation have passed, but when so, their successors survive as worthy of "ethnic observation." Still, my limited, parochial surveillance here would hardly constitute credibility because of their smaller sampling *vis à vis* the incredibly vaster numbers of immigrants who are incorporated in the above pages.

Concerning our numbers: From "Franco-american Oral Histories," About 11.8 million U.S. residents are of this [French] descent, of whom the majority are of French Canadian descent, and about 1.6 million speak French at home. An additional 450,000 U.S. residents speak a French-based creole language, according to the 2000 census.

On a regional basis at least (State of Maine and New England), how coincidental then, and strikingly helpful, it was to come across in my research a most credible document dated exactly one hundred years later (2012): *Franco-Americans in Maine and New England: Statistics from the American Community Survey* (prepared per the request of the State of Maine Legislative Franco-American Task Force

— James Myall, Consultant — from data collected by the United States Census Bureau). It is hoped that the following paraphrased extrapolations will whet your appetite to read the entire report (way below).

The transcript includes aggregated statistics of those respondents who identified as either French, French Canadian, Franco-Americans and French-Americans (assuming that the proportion of respondents who are immigrants — or descendants of immigrants — from France is small).

- In the State of Maine, the largest single ethnic group identifies as of French extraction.

- In New England it is the third-largest ethnic group that identifies as Franco-American. However the situation is "top-heavy" geographically. Whereas in Maine, New Hampshire, and Vermont Franco-Americans make up the largest ethnic group (a plurality), in Southern New England (Connecticut, Massachusetts, and Rhode Island), they form a simple minority.

- Franco-Americans are younger than non-Francos in any of the Northern New England states. This is despite an older audience for Franco-American events and outreach programs (e.g., Church?). Again, this youth trend is not borne out in Massachusetts, Connecticut, and Rhode Island.

- Statistics cited for only Maine include that family size for Franco-Americans is only slightly larger than that of other Mainers (a drastic contradiction of their past); Catholic traditions appear to be in decline when marital status is considered since the divorce rate is neither more or less likely for Mainers as a group; the fertility rate is slightly higher among Franco-American women; finally, more births were to unmarried Franco couples than to all Maine couples.

- Franco-Americans in Maine are less likely to graduate from high school than non-Francos, and less likely to achieve a higher education degree. At the high-school level, this pattern is repeated in New Hampshire and Vermont, but — again — not in Connecticut, Massachusetts and Rhode Island – in fact, in Southern New England, Franco-Americans are slightly *more likely* to graduate from high school. Further, in all of New England, Francos are not significantly less likely to be *currently* enrolled in colleges.

- The French language is no longer central to Franco identity although Maine stands out as having the highest rate of bilingualism of all New England states.

- Francos reflect the trends of Maine as a whole; and they are more likely to be involved in sales, production and natural resource-based occupations. (Reflection of the general lack of education among Francos.) They are more likely to remain in the labor force, enjoy a higher median *household* income but lower retirement and social security income.

Contrary to their history as an immigrant group, 98.5% of Franco-Americans today are native-born Americans.

After highlighting trends of that report, as I did above, there is indeed an inclination to conclude that Franco-Americans' evolvement or involvement in this geographic area at least has been rather lackluster. Perhaps as a former educator, the low number of high school graduates especially stings my Franco pride. (As for the rest, I will leave it to professional statisticians to surgically glean all of the thought-provoking inferences in the data about a people who trend younger than non-Francos, birth same-sized families, and survive the same volume of painful divorces.)

But hold on here; wasn't it Prime Minister Benjamin Disraeli (and later Mark Twain) who quipped, "There are three kinds of lies: lies, damned lies, and statistics." Bottom line: the Franco "lackluster" lies not at all in Myall's statistical report which, fulfilling its mission, is virtually an engaging *snapshot* of today; what is lacking according to my own paradigm here, it seems, is the historical context of this intriguing information. In other words, let's frame that snapshot.

Regarding education, for example, we must tack on the realization that it was only an average of two generations ago that our 1912 Franco-American ancestor-immigrants came to this country as peasants — mostly agricultural workers *(habitants)* — with much common sense and know-how, but lacking formal education. In the relatively-short distance they traveled here to become Americans, they necessarily, if fervently, faced the challenges of huge strides: a new language, new vocations, new social settings, a new culture and much prejudice. The following from the Maine Memory Network (mainememory.net): "The Maine State Legislature made it illegal to speak French in public schools (outside of foreign language lessons) in 1919, a law that persisted for half a century. Writing, 'I will not speak French in school' repeatedly was a common punishment for Francos in this period." Did the Legislature then simply believe that the French language displaced other learning? And that supposition seems kinder than others that come to mind. Again, I did not learn to speak French until I entered the first grade. *Au contraire*, mon frère, my French vocabulary did not impede learning. It motivated me to enhance it by translating to English. (How do you spell "assimilation?") To a large extent, education is a fungible, bequeathed value.

Secondly, the report translucently illustrates that the lesser levels of formal education for Francos seem more a matter of geography than of a lack of character. Here my mind leaps to the drastic differences between stats for the northern states of Maine, New Hampshire, and Vermont and those of Rhode Island, Massachusetts, and Connecticut. Perhaps this relates to a preference of continuing to live north in the comforting folds of one's tribe or clan and living close to the earth, perhaps a lack of propensity for risk-taking or of opportunity.

I take "artistic license" here and switch from geography to history. Project Muse, a leading provider of digital humanities and social science content for the scholarly community, claims:

> The historical experience of the French-Canadian presence in the United States is understudied. Franco-Americans, the descendants of French Canadian immigrants, have been less eager than members of other ethnic groups to investigate their past, and this hesitation has undoubtedly slowed the pace of both

amateur and professional enthusiasm for this topic. Within the past few years this situation has begun to change. Serious scholarly work on the Franco-American experience has been underway for the past two decades. And, with the publication of Gerard J. Brault's carefully documented and accessible study, *The French-Canadian Heritage in New England*, we have a state-of-the-art over-view which aims to provide an introduction to Franco-American studies for specialists and non-specialists alike.

In other words, so relatively little is recorded that we don't really know what we don't know. We might almost conclude, as Tevye did, "I don't knowl"

The demise of the culture itself? Inevitable! As Marianopolis College attests ("Quebec History: French Canadian Emigration to the United States 1840 – 1930): " On an internal level, the decline of Franco-America can chiefly be attributed to the decline of the textile industry in New England and to the social rise of Franco-Americans. American life and culture seduced younger Franco-Americans who realized that assimilation [including education and relocation] was the key to social improvement."

Thankfully, most Franco-Americans did not intentionally compromise their ethnic identity by changing their surname so as to nominally blend in with the peoples of other nationalities. Empirically, there can be no denying that today they/we are well-integrated into all aspects and levels of

American life. Only two generations later, read our vowel-impregnated surnames on the national, state, and municipal levels even though we collectively continue to maintain that "Quiet Presence" Dyke Hendrickson writes about in his book of the same title.

For the most part, as previously stated, we did not "lose our culture." We can hardly feel victims or cry "foul." It was barter: we admittedly forfeited it to share in the American Dream. Yet few of us would reverse the situation because we realize the enormous gains we have made on several levels, and — anyhow — we *know* who we are.

Notwithstanding some of our psychological and intellectual homogeneity with non-Francos, it is important to delineate that, here and there, there still are stark characteristics that define the Franco-American persona. A barroom generalization is the following: romantic, passionate, festive, industrious, neat, affectionate, and often possessed of Emerson's "Common Sense." Very much resembling the characteristics of southwestern people of Europe, e.g., Spaniards, Italians, etc. Often lacking the Anglo reserve — sometimes downright bawdy.

Allow me to revert 360 degrees back to "Growing Up..." After considerable reflection, I deduce that my own family seems a Franco-American microcosm of what appears to be a regional if not national trend.

With my dad's favorite den painting staring us in the face every day, "Success is health, one wife, and five degreed children," we were well-acquainted with the fact that school was the ticket *de rigeur*. Some of us took painful detours, but all of us did finally earn that degree. In an effort to capitalize on their investment, all of my siblings replicated the regional/national trend: went to school, relocated and did well. Not moi (relocation).

So true: French is a language we felt most comfortable speaking with our parents. Their passing keenly reduced the opportunity or challenge of maintaining that language. One local revival attempt was "The Rusty French Club" which was always well-attended because of the instructor's linguistic skills and creativity (former French instructor). Since my parents insisted we speak French "in the house," all of my siblings understand a French conversation, and they are likely to break into old bromides of same intermittently (often comically). One of my brothers and I often write in French on-line; you should see the reaction of "Spell Check!" It's such a kick to translate literally our parents' French idioms into English. (You had to be there!)

But just as most Francos today, most of our children (third generation) are not that proficient in the French language although my son, Christopher, perhaps because he is the eldest, if not profusely conversant, is most able to express himself speaking it here or abroad. One Quebec/Canadian nephew speaks French eloquently! Somewhat clinging to my Franco ethnicity, I will sometimes inquire of a younger person with a French surname, " Parles-tu français?" Most common response: "Not really, but I can understand some of it."

As the report suggests, trends in family life definitely point to a decline in the religiosity of many Francos and in the influence of the Catholic Church. This is perhaps the most attestable trait if considered both in our family and by attendance at our Church. Of nine grandchildren, I believe only three (with some of their spouses) attend Mass regularly although my son insists on joining me there whenever he visits. To further corroborate this diminution of Catholicism (across all nationalities actually) is the recognition that there are rarely communicants who are under forty years of age who regularly come to our churches.

> So what does it mean to be Franco-American today? Thankfully, the 1970s also saw the rise of institutions devoted to preserving Franco history and heritage... today's young Francos are re-discovering the culture of their grandparents. The days of neighborhoods filled with French voices may be over, but Franco culture survives, and is being embraced by a new generation. (Maine Memory Network)

As to what Franco-Americans have contributed, I again resort to Dyke:

> Those of French heritage have added a unique and vibrant accent to every community in which they have lived, and they are known as a cohesive ethnic group with a strong belief in family, church, work,

education, the arts, their language, and their community. Today they hold posts in every facet of Maine life, from hourly worker to the U.S. Congress. These hardworking people have a notable history and have been a major force in Maine's development.

Personally speaking, I dare to preface the following with Oprah's credo, "What I Know For Sure:"

That is to profoundly acknowledge that I and many of my Franco-American relatives, friends, and acquaintances, however happily steeped in the American way of life, are at times or perhaps even often intermittently harkened back to our Franco traditions. Think Marcel Proust and his "moments privilégiés" when coming upon a simple flower or hearing a certain sound brings you all the way back to the past. "Involuntary autobiographical memory," he named it, that occurs when cues encountered in everyday life evoke recollections of the past without conscious effort.

I cannot adequately describe the very real Franco-American remnant characteristics that our family (as in many other Franco homes) exudes whenever we gather. Indeed, it is a culture that we celebrate through our words, our food, our affection for each other, and for the breathtaking numbers of parental remembrances in which we unconsciously find ourselves. "Mom would love this!" - tourtières, belle maison, chanson. (Pork pies, beautiful home, song) Or "As Dad used to say, "Fait pas chaud dehors." (It's not warm out there.)

According to author, Gerard J. Brault, "culture" here being defined as a quality which one cannot always measure, compare, or otherwise quantify but which must be experienced. Culture is...a matter of the heart. It is the enrichment one *feels*.

In the very mill towns that originally attracted these immigrants, one can still overhear in a department store now and then remnants of the beautiful language that is French. While Catholic schools were far more numerous in the past, there are many flourishing today who earn national accreditation (NEASC!) for their excellence in leading a secular curriculum, but also intermittently weaving in that accredited academia some of the same Franco ideology/culture/norms from which their parents drew spiritual strength.

Starting on or about Thanksgiving through New Year's, that delicious aroma of pork pies baking in the oven is a Pavlov moment! Alert Hallmark!

Finally, there is the common denominator liturgy of our Church (where we are most likely to congregate), especially on first-class feasts (when attendance soars and the occasion becomes as much sociological as spiritual) and the pungent smell of incense arising in the sanctuary is somehow transformed into an anthem of the spirit for our faith community. Surely, our parents are smiling down at our traditions.

Silently, many of us reflect, "Je me souviens." **

~ FIN ~

** Motto of the Province of Quebec: I remember.

Franco-Americans in Maine:

Statistics from the American Community Survey

Prepared for the Franco-American Taskforce September 26, 2012

James Myall

Introduction:

As per the request of the State of Maine Legislative Franco-American Task Force, the following is an analysis of the Franco-American population in Maine from data collected by the United States Census Bureau. Before proceeding to analysis of the data, a few considerations must be highlighted.

About the American Community Survey:

The American Community Survey (ACS) is an annual survey conducted by the US Census Bureau to provide a broader snapshot of American life than is possible through the decennial census. The statistics gathered by the ACS are used by Congress and other agencies to determine the needs of Federal, State and local populations and agencies. The ACS is collected from randomly selected populations in every state to provide estimates which reflect American society as a whole.

The data for this report was taken from the ACS using the online tool of the US Census Bureau, American Factfinder, <http://factfinder2.census.gov>. This report largely relies on the 2010 1-year survey. For information on Maine's counties and on other New England states, the 5-year survey is used (longer- term estimates are allow analysis of smaller population units). Although the ACS surveys all Americans, the website allows users to filter data by several categories, including ancestry and ethnic origin, thus allowing a comprehensive picture of the Franco population. Where possible, I have added US Census Bureau data on Maine as a whole, for comparison.

'French' and 'French Canadian':

The US Census Bureau's ACS poses the question "What is this person's ancestry or ethnic origin?" It is important to note that the ACS question has several limitations. The most important is that the ACS does not provide discrete answers from which the respondent can choose. Because the question is open-ended, respondents to the ACS in Maine are divided between those who selected 'French' as their ancestry and those who selected 'French Canadian.' Since respondents who identified as French outnumber those who identified as French Canadian by a ratio of more than 2:1, it can be reasonably surmised that many of the 'French' respondents were, in fact, of French-Canadian origin.

Therefore, this report will include aggregated statistics of those respondents who identified as either French or French Canadian. The data will necessarily include both Franco-Americans and French- Americans (a distinction which the Taskforce may or may not wish to draw), but it is reasonable to assume that the proportion of respondents who are immigrants (or descendents of immigrants) from France is small.

A second issue raised by the use of ACS data is that it depends on respondents to self-identify as Franco- Americans. Therefore, this data can only be said to refer to self-identifying Franco-Americans. On the other hand, one could argue that any survey of an ethnic group would have this limitation.

Additionally, respondents were only permitted to choose a single ancestry or ethnic group in response to this question. So the data necessarily excludes the population of mixed Franco ancestry, most notably those who may identify more strongly as Irish-Americans or Métis (mixed French and American Indian).

For simplicity, I will use the data for the combined 'French' and 'French Canadian' responses, referring to them below as 'Franco-Americans'

Data for non Franco-Americans was calculated by subtracting the numbers for 'French' and 'French Canadian' respondents from the numbers reported for all Mainers.

Highlights:

The ACS divides its data into several demographic, social and economic categories. In many of these, it can be seen that Franco-Americans are not significantly different than Mainers as a whole. However, there are several points of data which bear highlighting. Charts and tables for these data are each included in the appendix.

Demographics

Those who responded as Franco-Americans numbered 321,994; of which 220,994 (16.6%) responded as 'French', and 101,004 (7.6%) as 'French Canadian. This represents 24.3% of Maine's population – the largest single ethnic group in the state (those identifying themselves as 'English' comprised 21.6%; 'Irish' 17.5%, and 'American' 8.2%)

Franco-Americans comprise significant populations across many of Maine's counties. They make up the smallest proportion of the population in Down East and Mid-Coast counties (Hancock, Washington, Waldo, Knox, Lincoln). This is to be expected of a population group that immigrated to Maine from the Northwest. In two counties – Aroostook and Androscoggin, the Franco-American population comprises over 30% of the total.

Across the state, Franco-Americans are concentrated in six counties – York, Cumberland, Androscoggin, Penboscot,

Kennebec and Aroostook. These six counties account for 78% of all Maine's Franco- Americans, and the top three counties – York, Cumberland and Androscoggin, for nearly half (47%). With the exception of Aroostook County, this reflects the historic pattern of immigration by Francos – Americans to industrial areas – especially Biddeford Saco (York Co.), Brunswick (Cumberland Co.); Lewiston-Auburn (Androscoggin Co.); Bangor (Penobscot Co.); Augusta and Waterville (Kennebec Co.). This distribution suggests that Franco-Americans have not greatly dispersed from these historic immigration centers.

Franco-Americans are younger than non-Francos. Maine's median age in 2010 was 42.7 years; Franco- Americans had a median age of 39.1 years, significantly lower than that of non-Francos, which was 43.7 years. This is despite an older audience for Franco-American events and outreach programs.

This statistic may be attributed to a slightly higher birth rate among Franco-Americans (see 'family' below). In addition, it seems likely that younger people, and those with children, are more likely to identify as being Franco-American.

Family

The average family size for Franco-Americans is slightly larger than that of other Mainers. Contrary to historical trends, Franco-American families are now of similar sizes to the average – Franco families contain an average of 2.91 people, while the state-wide average is 2.90 (there is a margin of error of 0.13).

Catholic traditions appear to be similarly in decline when we consider marital status – Franco-Americans are neither more nor less likely to be divorced than Mainers as a group. 14.1% of Franco-Americans were divorced, compared to 13.7% of Mainers as a group – once again, this is within the margin of error (of 2.11%).

The fertility rate is slightly higher among Franco-Americans women. Of all women aged 15 to 50, 5.35% had given birth in the past year, compared to 4.62% of Mainers as a whole. This would seem to reinforce the impression given by the marginally larger family size for Franco-Americans.

It is also possible that Franco-Americans are more likely to give birth while unmarried – 43.3% of births were to unmarried couples, as opposed to 36.6% of births among all Maine couples. However, this finding is problematic, due to the high margin of error in these statistics (16.5%, due to a very small sample size).

Education and Employment

In several categories, Franco Americans under-perform educationally compared to Mainers as a group. Franco-Americans are especially less likely to hold a bachelor's degree or higher qualification. Only 21.1% of Francos hold such qualifications, compared to 28.5% of all Mainers.

However, the data for educational enrollment reveals that Franco-Americans are not significantly less likely to be *currently* enrolled in education at the college level – 27.9% compared to 28.2% - which suggests that this deficit in college education is a hang-over from an earlier era in which college enrollment was low among Francos.

In terms of employment, Francos reflect the trends of the state as a whole. The exception is that Franco-Americans are slightly less likely to be engaged in management, business or service occupations, and more likely to be involved in sales, production, and natural resource-based occupations. This may be a reflection of the general lack of education among Franco-Americans.

Reflecting historical trends, Franco-Americans are slightly more likely to be engaged in farming or manufacturing than their peers statewide. The increased proportion of Francos engaged in farming, agriculture and fishing may be a result of the clustering of Franco populations in the Saint John Valley in rural Aroostook County. The marginally larger proportion of Francos engaged in manufacturing reflects a real change from historical trends, in which these jobs were the mainstay of the community. This is probably the consequence of the general decline in manufacturing in the state – it now represents only 8.8% of all jobs; 10.5% of Franco occupations (within the margins of error).

Franco-Americans are more likely to remain in the labor force than non-Francos. 36.2% of non-Francos aged 16 and over were out of the labor force in 2012; for Francos this figure was only 33.2% Franco- Americans are more likely to be employed (61.1% of the over-16 population) or unemployed (5.6%) compared to non-Francos (58.2% and 5.2% respectively). This is probably accounted for by the lower median age of Franco-Americans, but perhaps also by a stronger work ethic and reluctance to fully retire.

Mean earnings for Franco-Americans are lower, but comparable to those of Mainers - $58,014 to $61,648 – while the Median household income is higher among Franco-Americans. This represents a relatively small number of low-earning Franco-Americans skewing the mean earnings negatively. The higher median income shows that in many cases, Franco-Americans earn a little more than their peers in other Maine communities.

Mean retirement income and social security income is lower for Francos. Retired Franco-Americans earn $16,164 compared to Mainers' $19,984, or 80.9%. This reflects an historical trend towards lower earnings for Franco-Americans, which adversely affected their Social Security contributions.

Immigration

Contrary to their history as an immigrant group, Franco-Americans more likely to be native-born as other Mainers. 98.5% of Franco-Americans were native-born Americans, as were 95.9% of all Mainers.

Among the foreign-born Franco population, Franco-Americans are more likely to be naturalized. 66% of foreign-born Francos are naturalized, compared to 55% of other foreign-born Mainers. This is explainable due to Canadians' proficiency with English, and the length of stay of most Franco immigrants.

Franco-American immigration is mostly an historic phenomenon. As above, only 1.48% of all Franco- Americans are foreign-born; and these 4,778 immigrants represent just 10.5% of the total number of foreign-born Mainers. The data also show that 88.0% of Franco immigrants arrived in the United States before 1990.

Language

The French language is no longer central to Franco identity. Of those 5 years and older, who identified as Franco-American, only 12.3% of respondents said that they spoke a language other than English, presumably French. Furthermore, only

2.3% of respondents reported that they spoke English 'less than very well' (i.e. were monolingual Francophones). This still reflects a greater openness to foreign languages than non-Francos, 4.9% of whom speak a language other than English, and 1.5% of whom speak English 'less than very well'.

Conclusions

The findings from this analysis of the 2010 American Community Survey refute a number of preconceptions and stereotypes that are widely held among the non-Franco community. By and large, they also show deviations from historical trends among the Franco community, especially in regards to family, work and language. However, the data do highlight that access to education, especially adult education, is still a concern in this community.

Given that the US Census bureau is forbidden from asking questions about a person's religious convictions, this is perhaps the biggest omission from this analysis. Although trends in family life suggest a decline in the religiosity of many Francos and a decline in the influence of the Catholic Church, further study is needed to confirm this suspicion. It would also be helpful to study the effects of some of these changes to Franco society, especially their political affiliations. Overall, however, the study shows that self-identified Franco-Americans are still a significant group in the state, and one that is economically and demographically vibrant.

Franco-Americans in New England:

Statistics from the American Community Survey

Prepared for the Franco-American Taskforce October 24, 2012

Introduction:

As per the request of the State of Maine Legislative Franco-American Task Force, the following is an analysis of the Franco-American population in New England from data collected by the United States Census Bureau. This report accompanies 'Franco-Americans in Maine', which was also delivered to the Task Force, and is designed to determine whether the trends visible in Maine's Franco-American population are reflected in other New England states (i.e. Connecticut, Massachusetts, New Hampshire, Rhode Island and Vermont). Information concerning methodology is repeated below for the sake of completeness.

About the American Community Survey:

The American Community Survey (ACS) is an annual survey conducted by the US Census Bureau to provide a broader snapshot of American life than is possible through the decennial census. The statistics gathered by the ACS are used by Congress and other agencies to determine the needs of

Federal, State and local populations and agencies. The ACS is collected from randomly selected populations in every state to provide estimates which reflect American society as a whole.

The data for this report was taken from the ACS using the online tool of the US Census Bureau, American Factfinder, <http://factfinder2.census.gov>. This report largely relies on the 2010 5-year survey, which allows analysis of smaller population units than the 1-year survey which is more accurate. Although the ACS surveys all Americans, the website allows users to filter data by several categories, including ancestry and ethnic origin, thus allowing a comprehensive picture of the Franco population. Where possible, I have added US Census Bureau data on Maine, for comparison.

'French' and 'French Canadian':

The US Census Bureau's ACS poses the question "What is this person's ancestry or ethnic origin?" It is important to note that the ACS question has several limitations. The most important is that the ACS does not provide discrete answers from which the respondent can choose. Because the question is open-ended, respondents to the ACS in Maine are divided between those who selected 'French' as their ancestry and those who selected 'French Canadian.' Since respondents who identified as French outnumber those who identified as French Canadian by a ratio of more than 2:1, it can be reasonably surmised that many of the 'French' respondents were, in fact, of French-Canadian origin.

Therefore, this report will include aggregated statistics of those respondents who identified as either French or French Canadian. The data will necessarily include both Franco-Americans and French- Americans (a distinction which the Taskforce may or may not wish to draw), but it is reasonable to assume that the proportion of respondents who are immigrants (or descendents of immigrants) from France is small.

A second issue raised by the use of ACS data is that it depends on respondents to self-identify as Franco- Americans. Therefore, this data can only be said to refer to self-identifying Franco-Americans. On the other hand, one could argue that any survey of an ethnic group would have this limitation.

Additionally, respondents were only permitted to choose a single ancestry or ethnic group in response to this question. So the data necessarily excludes the population of mixed Franco ancestry, most notably those who may identify more strongly as Irish-Americans or Métis (mixed French and American Indian).

For simplicity, I will use the data for the combined 'French' and 'French Canadian' responses, referring to them below as 'Franco-Americans'

Data for non Franco-Americans was calculated by subtracting the numbers for 'French' and 'French Canadian' respondents from the numbers reported for all Mainers.

Highlights:

The ACS divides its data into several demographic, social and economic categories. This report focuses on those categories in which Franco-Americans displayed statistical differences from non-Francos in Maine. In particular these were *educational attainment* and *bilingualism*. For reference purposes, some basic information on Franco-American *identity, age* and *population distribution* across New England States was also included.

Population

In total, some 2,041,387 New Englanders identify as Franco-American. This represents some 11.5% of the region's population. This makes Franco-Americans the third-largest ethnic group in New England, behind Irish Americans (16.22%) and Italian Americans (11.21%).

However, the situation varies greatly in individual states. States in Southern New England – Connecticut, Massachusetts and Rhode Island – contain more than half of New England's Franco-Americans (1,258,237, or 61.6%), but make up relatively small populations *within* each of these states (8.7%, 11.8% and 16.6% respectively).

In Northern New England, by contrast – Maine, New Hampshire and Vermont – Franco-Americans make up the largest ethnic group. This difference between Southern New England, in which Francos form a minority, and Northern New England, where they form a plurality, highlights a difference which is repeated in other categories.

Identity

As in Maine, Franco-Americans in New England describe themselves variously as 'French' or 'French Canadian' (see note on the ACS methodology above). In every state, the responses were divided similarly. Respondents described themselves as 'French' twice as often as they did 'French Canadian'. This reinforces the theory that these respondents could be described with confidence as Franco- Americans and not, for the most part, French-Americans.

Age

In Maine, Franco-Americans tend to be younger than non-Francos (39.1 years, compared to 43.7 years). Maine's trend is repeated in the other Northern New England states, but not in the Southern part of the region. In fact, Franco-Americans in Maine, New Hampshire and Vermont are younger than their non- Franco neighbors *and* younger than their compatriots in Massachusetts, Connecticut and Rhode Island.

Educational Attainment

The task force was particularly concerned that Maine's Franco-Americans were underperforming educationally. Franco-Americans in Maine are less likely to graduate from high school than non-Francos, and less likely to achieve a higher education degree. At the high-school level, this pattern is repeated in New Hampshire and Vermont, but not in Connecticut, Massachusetts and Rhode Island – in fact, in Southern New England, Franco-Americans are slightly *more likely* to graduate from high school.

Franco-Americans in Maine suffer from the highest rate of failure to graduate high school than many of the groups examined (11.5%; Rhode Island's rate for Franco-Americans is 14%), yet this is probably due to factors affecting all Mainers. The difference between Franco-Americans and non-Francos is in fact smaller in Maine than in New Hampshire and Vermont. Maine's Franco-Americans are 26% more likely to have less than a high school education than their non-Franco peers; in New Hampshire and Vermont, Franco-Americans are 31% and 32% more likely, respectively.

In terms of higher education, Franco-Americans in all states underachieve compared to non-Franco- Americans. Generally, in southern New England, Franco-Americans are between 20% and 28% less likely to achieve a Bachelor's degree or higher than non-Francos. In Northern New England, the difference is greater – between 26% and 46%. As with high school graduation rates, Maine has the second-lowest proportion of Franco-Americans with 4-year degrees (21.1%, the rate for Francos in Vermont is 20%). However, the difference in the proportion of the population holding 4-year degrees is less between Maine's Franco-Americans and non-Francos than in other states, especially compared to the other New England states.

Bilingualism

In this category, Maine stands out as having the highest rate of bilingualism of all New England states. 12.3% of Maine Franco-Americans over the age of five report speaking a language in addition to English, compared to approximately half that rate in other New England states. Some of this difference may be accounted for by the Acadian population in the St John Valley region of Aroostook County, in which French is particularly widely spoken.

Conclusions

In general, this report confirms that many of the findings of *Franco-Americans in Maine* are common to Franco-Americans across New England. That would suggest that the causes of these trends are indeed due to experiences and factors unique to Franco-Americans.

A clear divide emerges between northern New England states in which Franco-Americans make up an ethnic plurality (Maine, New Hampshire and Vermont), and Southern New England, where they are one of many minorities (Connecticut, Massachusetts, and, to a lesser extent, Rhode Island). In the northern New England states, Franco-Americans tend to be younger, and less well-educated, both compared to non-Francos in those states, and in comparison to their compatriots in southern states. These two phenomena may well be linked: the lower median age for Franco-Americans is probably accounted for by a higher birth rate, and lower education levels tend to correlate to higher birth rates.

Although it is not evidenced by this report, it would be a reasonable assumption that Franco-Americans in Southern New England are 'assimilated' (to use the word cautiously) to a greater extent than those in Northern New England. Franco-Americans in these states, forming only one of many minority groups, may have faced less historic discrimination, and have greater educational aspirations and opportunities. However, more research will be needed to support such a conclusion.

~ Works Cited ~

"Our Story." *Bates Mill Store,* batesmillstore.com/pages/our-story, accessed 14 February, 2017

Brault, Gerard J. *The French-Canadian Heritage in New England*, UPNE, 1986

Carlyle, Thomas. "A Mechanical Age." *The Edinburgh Review 1802-1929*, edited by Francis Jeffrey, published by Archibald Constable, 1829

Doiron, Paul. "Lingua Franca." *Down East Magazine,* December, 2015

"Grand Trunk Railroad Station (Lewiston)," *en.wikipedia. org/wiki/Grand_Trunk_ Station,* accessed 14 February, 2017

Haley, Alan. "Demographics, Xenophobia Aren't Working in Our State's Favor," *Portland [Maine] Press Herald*, April 11, 2016

Castille, Connie and Bohl, Allison. "I Always Do My Collars First: a Film About Ironing," *Maine Routes*, 27 August, 2008

"Franco-American Oral Histories." *francoamericanarchives. org/about-nous-autres/franco-american-history/franco-ameri-can-americain/,* accessed 14 February, 2017

Hendrikson, Dyke. *Quiet Presence*, Gannett Press, Portland, 1980

_____ *Franco-Americans of Maine*, Arcadia Publishing Press, Charleston, South Carolina, 2010

Daunais, Isabelle. "Quebec Fiction – History and Criticism," *La Pratique du Roman*, Paper presented at McGill University, 2011

"Journal of Canadian Studies," *Project Muse*, Volume 50, University of Toronto Press, Toronto, 2016

Ledoux, Denis. "Germaine." *Maine Speaks: An Anthology of Maine Literature*, The Maine Writers and Publishers Alliance, 1989

Le F.A.R.O.G., umaine.edu/francoamerican/le-forum/, University of Maine

Levine, Linda. "Congressional Research Service," *The Labor Market During the Great Depression and the Current Depression,* 2009

Maine Secretary of State, "Politics," *Portland [Maine] Press Herald*, 2 June, 2014

Meunier, Laurie. "On Being Franco-American," *Wolf Moon Press/Journal:A Maine Journal of Art and Opinion*, April-May, 2003

Myall, James. "Franco-Americans in Maine and New England," *State of Maine Legislative Task Force,* 2012

_____ "From French Canadians to Franco-Americans," *Maine Memory Network,* mainememory.net, accessed 14 February, 2017

Pinette, Susan. "Teaching Franco-Americans of the Northeast." *The French Review*, 80:6, 2007, 1352-1360

Powers, John R. *Do Black Patent Leather Shoes Really Reflect Up?* Regnery, 1975

"The Victorian Age." *The Norton Anthology of English Literature,* Volume 2, M. H. Abrams, General Editor, W. W. Norton and Company, 1962